Spirit Baby

CHRISTINE NIGHTINGALE

ISBN-13: 978-15177 38570
ISBN-10:15177 38571

FEEDBACK FROM SPIRIT BABY CLIENTS

"Hi Christine,

Wow, the reading was AMAZING.....So much of it resonates with me, and I feel so much more at peace, and excited about all that came through! I'm so grateful that this world has people like you! Blessings, N. "

"Christine, Just wanted to let you know I am 12 weeks pregnant! With twins! Thanks for your help ,J."

Follow- up: Client sent me photos of two beautiful baby boys.

"Hi Christine ,

Thank you so much for an amazing reading! We are so grateful and feel blessed to have contacted you. You are very gifted . Words can't express how happy and relieved we feel and we can't thank you enough!!!!!! Much love and light ,A."

"Hi Christine,

I just wanted to share the news with you! I am 9 weeks pregnant with twins!!

Thank you for the session that we had back in March!!!

Best regards, Y"

"Dearest Christine, firstly thank you so very much for sending me my reading so quickly. It has bought such peace to my heart. What you have said has given me the key to free my mind and see the situation with a new found clarity and purpose. If I hadn't found you I really don't know how I would have come to terms with things as well as find the courage and strength to go on.

Christine, my gratitude is beyond words, for what you have given me; hope, faith, and the courage to trust my heart. The past I understand, I am at peace in the moment and the future is full of light and promise. I feel so lucky that I found you.

Thank you for being here and sharing your gift, thank you. Love and blessings."

"Thank you thank you! This reading has warmed my heart and is helping me to continue this journey and not give up. I have always felt a connection to the Spirit Baby and I will try to spiritually connect to him. Everything you have said I have known. I am grateful for you and your gift.

Blessings, S."

"Hi Christine,

Thank you so much for the Spirit Baby channeling which was lovely and so reassuring. Thank you for the advice . I am feeling a lot more positive about the whole process after your reading. It's a blessing I found your website. Keep doing the amazing work you're doing. Thank you again so much.

Angel Blessings, C."

"Dear Christine,

I can never thank you enough! The messages you shared with me assured me that my sweet child is there, and will soon be part of our family. The messages also confirmed what I already knew in my heart, that I can do this naturally!

Thank you for giving me back faith in my own body!
You are a very special human being. I am so happy that I found you! What an amazing gift you have!
Thank you again, you've restored my faith and given joy back to me!

Warmly, C. "

"Hi Christine,

We hope this message finds you, the cats, and chickens all well. I would like to cancel our meeting next week for the happiest of reasons. Everything is going very well. My husband and I are talking to the baby every day and best of all I'm feeling calm and relaxed. All of our early medical tests (blood and ultrasound) show that baby is developing well and all looks normal. We want to thank you for all that we learned in our earlier meetings and to thank you for your warmth and compassion.

(Follow up...client delivered a beautiful baby boy and came to see me for help contacting another spirit baby.)

Warmest Regards, M."

"Wow, Christine! I just read this- unbelievable! I awoke suddenly its 4 am here checked my phone. And found your email. Thank you so very much. You were right on the money, it's what I thought. So, happy to hear the baby is always with me. And really amazing you heard his voice. I knew he was a boy. I'm so happy to know he knew I loved him and wanted him. You are amazing. I feel better now but have to tell you, I'm still surprised. It's still sinking in."

"Thank you so much dearest Christine! I was so delighted to wake up this morning and receive your reading . It certainly explains a lot and brought tears to my eyes. This Spirit Baby sounds like such a joy and so perfect for me. I'm so inspired, to think of this beautiful life we will be able to have. Your reading was a gift to me in so many ways. I really can't thank you for it enough. We are blessed on this earth to have people like you, truly. I'll get to work with implementing your suggestions right away.

Kindest regards,

L "

"Exciting news - I'm pregnant!   We are beyond excited and I just wanted to reach out to you and let you know. It's funny, I woke up with this really good, really positive energy all around me and especially around my abdomen. I am convinced the spirit work and Reiki treatments you did contributed greatly to this outcome. I am continuing to meditate and talk to the babies every day and continue to visualize my uterus in a glowing pink color with healing white light inside. I also focus on my heart chakra a lot. Thank you so much for everything you have done Christine.
T"

"I appreciate your help, guidance, and love. Your words have brought me such peace. I now sing to and talk with my Spirit Baby often...and I know she hears me. I asked her for an obvious sign, that I needed to know it was her. A feather flew right into my hands the following day.... It wasn't a bird's feather, it wasn't a pillow feather, it was a feather like I have never seen. I knew it was her sign for me.

Thank you, Christine."

"Dear Christine,

Thank you for that beautiful response. It gives me strength and hope. I appreciated, too, the resources you included.

"Thank you so much for your response. You are an amazing human being for helping so many people and giving us hope.
Very grateful to you. Love "

"Christine,
 Thank you again for your accurate and insightful reading. I wanted to follow up on your suggestion for hypnosis and aromatherapy - I think it is absolutely correct that my body does not feel that it is "safe" to become pregnant and I'm working so hard at meditating, holistic living, trying to calm down/slow down, etc.
Your first reading on my Spirit Babies really made a big impact in my life and the way I've been thinking- and the more I try to open my 3rd eye and really listen, the more obvious it is to me that there is a presence in my life that is trying to get in contact with me- I want to put myself in a place where I can be open to receiving those messages, and your first reading certainly did that for me.
Best, L"

"Good morning Christine! I wanted you to know how much you have helped me since the reading. I have been meditating daily and communicating with ….. They have opened my heart up to forgiving myself and moving to a place of peace within myself. Oh what an incredible gift you have to see these things- . I am so very grateful for your gift!!!!!!! thank you from the bottom of my heart and soul! My life has become one of sheer joy from that place of such deep sorrow. I still miss …. in many ways and in many moments of each day....but in a different way. I feel her presence always. She has shown me many signs of her presence during each day. How may I repay you Christine? Is there anything I can say or do to give back to you even some of what you have given me/ our family /our marriage/ my ability to love others again. THANK YOU! THANK YOU! THANK YOU! With a hug and a huge appreciation...."

"I am now 7 months pregnant and doing follow-up work Super many many thanks Christine, you are an angel:-)))"

"Thank you very much for the reading Christine. I have

Just finished reading all of the attachments here, and I am going to read over the actual reading again to fully absorb all of the important info in there. I really appreciate this, and again thank you for allowing your gift to be shared with the world. There really is a lot to think about in that reading, so I need to sit here and think about it carefully, and soak it all in again. I am so glad that I have had this done, I can reflect back on this in my own way. I think I am still in awe with some of the info in this reading."

"Hello Christine, Thank you so much for the amazing reading with our Spirit Babies. Just some quick feedback. It never ceases to amaze me how Spirit works and guides in our lives - it is a constant reminder of the magic that surrounds us and how much we have to be grateful for. Your reading was wonderful confirmation for what I have been feeling for myself, and possibly doubting or resisting, about the direction in which to develop or work further. It is like being able to see where you are meant to be going, but step by step putting everything together like a puzzle and this has just provided one of the missing pieces. It brought just that extra peace of mind and clarity, that sometimes you can't quite find for yourself."

"Dear Christine,

I don't know whether you remember me, but you very kindly did a Spirit Baby reading for me just over a year ago. You gave me great hope; there was a boy and a girl waiting, which was compatible with what I myself had intuited. I conceived , as agreed with my spirit babies. I have so far enjoyed a healthy, uncomplicated pregnancy. I had an ultrasound scan at 22 weeks and all appeared well."

"Hi Christine I am happy to let you know that our daughter was born and we are both doing well:-) She is gorgeous, alert and smart and very sweet. .Many thanks again for your guidance and help, it meant a lot to me. I trust all is well with you and your family:-)Much love"

"Hi Christine!

Thank you for your response a couple of weeks ago! I wanted to update you that I just found out I'm pregnant!
 Only about 2-3 weeks along so it's still very early :)
I know my job is to continue singing to my Spirit Baby and shifting my anxiety, which I feel has made a huge difference in my energy.
Thank you!"

"Hi Christine, I've been meaning to get back to you for a very, very long time. A few days after I received this lovely reading I found out I was pregnant. We had a little boy who is the happiest baby I have ever known. Last week I found out I'm pregnant again - very much a bit of an oops on our part and not planned. I've been worrying a lot and dug out this reading to help calm the fears. I hope all is well with you and thanks again."

"Hi Christine this was so beautiful and meaningful. I am still taking it in. I am so grateful for your gift and your sharing it. I was fascinated by what you were able to gain from talking with our Spirit Baby. I am again so grateful for the insights. It felt quite specific and correct about what you said."

"Christine, I don' t know if you remember me. We worked together last....and after much work, I am now 8 weeks pregnant!"

"Our precious baby boy was born. I wanted to let you know how much your work helped me to heal and conceive right away. Everything your reading said made so much sense and I can tell that our boy is everything he communicated through you. Thank you so much for what you have done for us! Also as mentioned in the reading, Spirit Baby said that my sister's baby ... they had an agreement to come in together... well she is due in 4 months, so that is happening too!!

I attached a picture of our precious boy. I mentioned your work to .. and how it helped me. She wants to have a session.

Love and Happiness"

"Thanks so much Christine. The information and insight you have provided has helped to clarify and validate much of what I was feeling. Thank you for all the additional resources. Your gift is truly beautiful and I am so grateful for your assistance in helping me be one step closer to my baby to be :)"

"Thank you so much for your reading, the messages confirmed what I knew in my heart. I feel blessed to have contacted you, please keep doing the amazing work you are doing."

"Thank you so much, Christine! Thanks for the reading and for the other articles to help as I continue on my journey. All of this is appreciated beyond words. Hope you have a fantastic day. All the best."

"Hello Christine,

You are never going to believe this, but I just got a positive pregnancy test!!"

C: Sure, I believe it, that sort of thing happens often to my clients....
Establishing contact seems to stir things up ...

"WOOHOO! That is just amazing!!!Thank you!!! "

"Christine,

So lovely speaking with you.

Just found out today that we are pregnant again. How beautiful!

 Sending you much love."

"Hi Christine!

Just wanted to let you know that I am pregnant! I'm exactly 5 weeks. I think doing some of the things you suggested like visualization and meditation was really helpful."

"Thanks Christine! Wow wow wow!!!! Spot on and I'm still reading your response as the words keep changing form each time I read your words. I know about the environmental warriors and I knew about healing the world. I knew about the birthing method...I cried for joy … and I am feeling excited about teaching my cherubs :-)

I feel joy and I'm so glad I found you! I feel blessed!"

"Dear Christine,

Thank you very much for connecting with our spirit baby again. The reading is wonderful and very important to me. Thank you from the bottom of my heart.

Love,"

"Thanks so much for your lovely email! I always look forward to reading them. I'm feeling very powerful and more confident! This stuff is real and you helped me connect to my spirit babies!"

"Hi Christine,

It's been awhile, but I just wanted to say thank you again for your words of encouragement. My daughter was born in March 2014 and my son made an unexpected appearance in May this year. I hope that you're doing well.
with love and light,
C"

"I want to say thank you from the bottom of my heart for your services. The reading with my Spirit Baby was truly amazing! It served me as confirmation for what I had already felt but wasn't sure because I thought maybe it was me making up things. It truly helped me to be at peace and it made me feel truly connected to my Spirit Baby!!
Again thank you!"

This Book is dedicated to Walter Makichen , the warm and wonderful author of Spirit Babies. I was asked to channel him a month after his passing. It was made clear in that session that I could continue his work but "in my own way." Within a few months of that experience I retired from teaching and started working with parents who wanted to communicate with the spirits of their future children.

MY RELUCTANT GIFT

As with anyone else who finds they are working on their true Life Task, I can look back and see that I was perhaps being prepared for it all my life.

As a baby I had past life dreams . As a very young child I was aware of angels in the garden, and thought that talking to angels was no different than talking to your parents. My parents did not teach us about religion. My mother prayed in secret; my father was an agnostic.

When I was five I realized that the other members of my family were not aware of angels, past lives, or hands-on healing of sick or injured pets… and I decided to keep that understanding secret. I wanted nothing more than to have a "normal life", get married, have kids, and become a teacher.

I was rescued by angels twice. The first time I was about 9. We lived in the country in Northern Ontario, and had to take a school bus which stopped on the highway to pick us up. Our house was on a hill, and it was not possible to see what was coming over the hill; there were often accidents at that location, including a fatality.

My brother Ernie and I took our lives in our hands every time we crossed the highway to get home. On this occasion I had just started crossing when I saw a car bearing down upon me at highway speeds. I thought to myself, "I guess I am going to die."

Suddenly I felt myself being picked up and deposited by the side of the road. Nothing was visible. My brother Ernie said I spun away from the car like a top- he thought I had been hit, though there was not a mark on me. In fact of course a child hit by a car would have been thrown and possibly killed .

The second time I was in a crowded swimming pool, and I did not know how to swim. I held onto the wall along the side of the pool by the deep end and for some reason let go. As I was going down for the third time someone picked me up, deposited me on the side of the pool, and left without waiting to be thanked. I thought I heard a male voice asking if I was all right but I did not see anything.

It is generally believed by those who are spiritually inclined that if you are rescued from something which could have killed you, you have not yet completed what you came here to do. I believe that most adults have probably been rescued , but may not be aware of the fact that, for example, on the day they "decided to" take a different road home from work they avoided a car crash which could have killed them.

My youngest brother Frank was born when I was 7 and I remember thinking "'he's going to be my baby." I took a great interest in telling him his bedtime stories, playing with him, and we were always very close.

Many years later I channeled that around 1910 I had been a teenaged girl who died while she was pregnant. So the unfinished business of that lifetime led to our being siblings in this life, in which I got a chance to 'mother" him in a different way.

Frank and his girlfriend asked me (a few years ago) to channel how they had known each other before.

I learned that they were Innuit brothers in the north of Russia, one of them a shaman (my brother, I think)and one a hunter. In this lifetime his girlfriend is of Russian background. In this lifetime also my brother loves the far north, having spent every summer of his university years working in the Yukon. Again, past life circumstances impacted in this life, including the energy connection which brought the spirits of the former brothers together for a time .

On my first day of university I met a future lifelong friend. As we were standing in line to pick our courses I got a single-word intuitive message "brother". I knew that when someone had shared a past life with me, I would know that fact from the first time I looked into their eyes. The details would come back to me in time. But I did not seek to investigate this ability. I have never met anyone else who spontaneously remembers past lives (in my case about two dozen) and so it was one more thing I usually kept hidden.

David and I have been friends for 48 years, but I did not check the Akashic records for the details until decades after we met.

It turns out that he and I were indeed brother and sister, and the woman he later married had been our younger sister in that lifetime. The woman who became their nanny, and helped raise their children, had been our father (all souls have been attached to bodies of both genders.)

So as is often the case, there was a lot of past life business to attend to. David's life was very highly impacted by that lifetime. Past life connections are the basis of a great many relationships in everyone's life, affecting which souls will be our parents, children, siblings, friends, and partners.

At teacher's college one of my friends started having kids early...two boys, then a girl. I thought that was perfect, and decided I would do the same. (I did not have the concepts at that time to understand that my three spirit babies were already in my aura and that this would determine who was eventually born to me.) I sewed Dorothy a layette...a complete set of baby clothes ...as I always had a soft spot for babies. (I have made gifts for every baby at the local woman's shelter for 9 years.)

When I became a teacher my intuition was of great help to me. One of my principals said I was better at knowing what made kids tick, and explaining it to others, than anyone else she knew. That was high praise.... and I attribute it to my intuitive understanding.

I always felt that the universe went to a lot of trouble to make sure that a kid who had fallen through the cracks ended up in my class. The other kids in the class would have been fine with any other teacher.

So it was that I was assigned a student in fourth grade who was believed to be unintelligent, as her language skills were very low. But her beautiful drawings showed me that she was very capable. Within a few days I realized that she was deaf! The following year she was transferred into a classroom for the hearing impaired.

There was another student in my grade four class who was described to me as lazy and badly behaved. Within a few days I determined that his atrocious spelling and handwriting were signs of a learning disability ...yet his sense of humor indicated good understanding. So he was apparently gifted/learning disabled... a much more common situation than most people realize. Such children would rather be perceived as "bad" than "dumb."

With this understanding and the help of his classmates it was possible to turn my student's life around. I made him my classroom attendance monitor, which made it possible to have a few minutes each day to talk to his classmates about how we could help him. Strategy one: he was allowed to have one of the two computers in the classroom, which took care of the handwriting and spelling problems. Strategy two: all the children agreed to completely ignore him when he misbehaved, which took care of the acting-out. Very soon our classroom community got him to like himself and to behave appropriately .

When the Toronto Sun later did a feature piece on the writing of my students, this child's poem on what it felt like to have a learning disability was one of the works which was published .

The best years of teaching (in over 30 years) were those with a very high needs group of children, multiply challenged, in wheelchairs. I found that I was able to reach them intuitively even if they were non–verbal. I felt a strong calling to teach that class …a meaningful "coincidence".

Our major challenges are arranged for us by the universe to develop our capacities so that we can fulfill our Life Tasks. And those Special Needs children had in some cases... maybe all... chosen their challenges.

It was my conscious choice to refrain from talking about my intuitive abilities for about 40 years. This meant that although I got past life glimpses and intuitive understanding about my students, and certainly a lot of intuitive information about siblings, partners, friends and my own three children, I did not discuss this .

It wasn't until I was 46 that I felt a great pull to start to understand what I had always known. I heard the word Reiki , for example, and immediately knew that it was for me... even though I had no idea what it involved. (Reiki is a form of hands-on healing which involves clearing blockages from the energy system or chakras.)

As soon as I became a Reiki Master and started seeing clients, I received messages from spirits in their auras. For example a woman got a message from a spirit who identified herself as my client's Nikomis. The client had not told me that she was of First Nations heritage. Nikomis is a native word for grandmother .

I encountered the legacy of Spirit Babies in the auras of two women over 50 who had had terminations. In one case the girl spirit said it had been her Life Task to help her mother throughout her life. She had not had the opportunity to successfully communicate to date (two other babies were born to the woman with a later husband) but the Spirit Baby had chosen to stay in her mother's aura. She asked her mother if it would be possible to start communication now. The client agreed.

In the second case the woman had had two terminations prior to having her son. The girls were no longer in her aura, but her higher self said that the client needed to know that the spirits were still in her family. Her brother had become a father to twin girls, to whom my client said she was very attached.

I studied a great many healing modalities, starting in 1996. Some of the more useful for me included Hypnosis, Aromatherapy, and Reiki. But when spiritual things were explained, none of it was new to me; I had always known most of what was addressed, though I had not discussed it before.

Past Life Regression intrigued me, as I have had past life memories all my life. I found that I was able to channel past lives for my clients. (Probably anyone can learn how to channel; it involves picking up information that is part of The Field or All That Is. It is not based on either study or sensory input.)

A young man came in to see me for a Reiki treatment, saying he was unable to work due to pain in his back and upper shoulder areas. I immediately became aware of two past life images. One was of an Innuit stone carver. The other was of a Confucian calligrapher. I invited my client to tell me what he thought these two past lives had in common. (They were obviously related to his psychic pain, which was expressing itself physically. Louise Hay talks about this concept in her excellent book, <u>You Can Heal Your Life</u>.)

My client said these were both creative people . I explained that his past incarnations were showing themselves to him to let him realize the reason for his dis-ease.

"When exactly did you start feeling this pain?" I asked him.

"When I agreed at the age of 15 to cave in to my parents' pressure… to give up my dreams of becoming an artist and become an engineer."

I told the young man he had some homework to do before I saw him again. He was to do a painting for me. He protested that he had not painted in ten years. Nevertheless I insisted that he do a painting .

I bought the painting from the young man (the first one he ever sold). It now hangs in my front hall. There is a large orange sun in one corner (representing his creative chakra opening). A lizard on a plant is crawling up towards the sun. Michael did not consciously know why he put in a feather floating down (in fact he did not understand any of the archetypal symbolism he had put into his own painting.) But I told him that his Innuit incarnation would have known the significance of finding a feather as a gift from spirit when a person is embarking on their true path. The young man called the painting Towards Freedom. He is a graphic artist now.

Studying past life regression hypnosis in 2002 gave me a deeper understanding of the channeling I had done with hundreds of clients over the years (picking up past life information and spirit messages). Everyone is capable of reliving their past lives in a trance state.(As I later discovered, it is also possible for mothers to communicate with their Spirit Babies in trance.)

I have known for many years that I had a past life as a shaman's daughter somewhere in the North Eastern United States. This teenaged girl lived largely in the forest, communing with the animals, returning to the tribe when she felt she was needed. At first contact her whole community was destroyed.

In my fifties I went to visit my older brother who lives in northern Maine. He recommended that I go for a walk on a popular hiking trail. I knew as I stepped onto it that this was exactly where I had once lived with my Native family, and that I was walking on a sacred trail. I was drawn to a huge boulder on the side of the path, put my hands on it and felt the deep, strong heartbeat of Mother Earth.

Upon returning to my brother's home and talking of the experience, I clairvoyantly saw his face change to native North American features…he had been a member of my tribe. It was clear to me why my brother Ernie had fallen in love with this setting as soon as he saw it as a young man, and had resolved to make his home there.

But I did not meet my former father from that lifetime until I took a course in hypnosis in 2008. Within a few days of meeting John, a fellow student, I shared my understanding that he had been my father when he was a native shaman.

John has made an intensive study of native spirituality although he was not born native in this life. He now leads drum circles at my home at the solstices and equinoxes.

I am currently studying Shamanism, as I understand that going to "see" clients all over the world, and communicate with their babies, is my form of shamanism. (The knowledge comes after the knowing…it is a matter of "re-membering" what one has always known…putting it back together.)

For many years I continued to teach while seeing one or two clients a week on the side.

One very powerful personal spirit message came from my beloved aunt Corrie. She had lived in Holland all her life, and never married. She was a sweet, selfless person who had spent her life working in a home for delinquent boys, who I am sure she helped enormously with her no-nonsense but loving approach.

As the one of five siblings who spoke Dutch most fluently, I was called by the hospital to notify us of her passing at age 90. I was busy for the next few hours notifying my far-flung brothers so we could all go to her funeral, when I felt a painful buzzing in my ear. This is sometimes the signal of a psychic message coming in. So I sat down to receive it .

Corrie's voice in the room very clearly said, in Dutch of course, 'Het liefde is de enige ding die belangrijk is:'" (Love is the only thing that matters.)

A major change in my life trajectory came in April of 2011. I was taking an advanced course in Hypnosis for Fertility. The instructor, Shawn , asked each student to tell something interesting about themselves. I said that I was able to channel. She asked, "Can you channel Walter?"

"Who's Walter?" I asked. Shawn mentioned his book Spirit Babies. I had read it but had not registered the author's name. "I can channel anyone who is willing and available to be channeled," I stated.

To say this was a life changing experience   would be an understatement. I asked, "Can I do what you have done?"

"Yes, but you will do it in your own way."

By October of 2011 I was seeing my first Spirit Baby clients. In January of 2012 I retired from teaching so I could dedicate more of my time to the hundreds of Spirit Baby clients who have since that time come my way. (If any of them mention Walter I feel he has sent them to me.)

I am dedicating this book to him.

Christine Nightingale,

B.A (Psychology), Teacher, Reiki Master, Certified Hypnotist, Aromatherapist, Spirit Baby communicator

CONTENTS

ACKNOWLEDGMENTS

To my son David, a very talented writer of science fiction and poetry who encouraged me to try to get my book published, and his lovely lady Carolyn.

To my "baby brother" Frank, a kind and gentle soul who is always a good listener.

To my lifelong friend David, whose sense of humour is a beacon of light, and who thought that getting my book "out there" was a great idea.

To my grandchildren Marquis, Lily, and Beatrix, who keep me in touch with the innocence and energy of extreme youth.

To my children Julie and Johnathan, and to Melissa, Amy and Dwayne, for bringing new children into my life.

To Johnathan also for doing an excellent job setting up and maintaining my website.

CHAPTER ONE : SIGNS AND SPIRIT BABIES

All of us are connected. Every living thing, every robin, every rock. Images we see in the natural world, or in our dreams, can therefore be important messages from our guides.

Native North American people say that our dreams can give warnings of possible futures; the aboriginals of Australia felt that Dreamtime was more real than the everyday world.

Spirit is in everything. A sign which comes from the environment-inner or outer-(not from a friend or adviser directly talking to you about a problem)- is a cledon. These synchronistic messages , arranged by guides and angels, may be recurring numbers, license plates with messages, signs on trucks, books , or overheard conversations which address your issue. Meaningful coincidences, such as three friends in one week telling you that you should read a book (or serendipitously learning of a new course just when you started investigating a new field of study) should be paid attention to. They have been arranged by your guides and angels.

When working with my clients who have had miscarriages, I encourage them to look for cledons in the environment (inner and outer). For example, it is believed in Japan that a spirit between lives can take the form of a butterfly.

1.) When I told this to a client, she excitedly told me that after her lost pregnancy, an unusual butterfly flew in to the house , landed on a curtain ,and stayed for several hours. She now understood that her miscarried baby was letting her know that she was coming back.

2.) Another client told me that as she was texting her husband (who was in a boat on the ocean, fishing with the client's father) he saw a butterfly, miles from shore, at the same time that my client noticed one in her garden.   (Spirit can be in two places at one time .)

3.) A client had suffered a stillborn baby boy. We worked at communicating with his spirit. Months later my client told me she was pregnant, and felt guilty and confused. The new baby was a girl, and my client only wanted her son back! I was able to tell her that souls are neither male nor female, and that her child was in fact the return of her stillborn son. Only then did the client remember a dream she had had , early in this pregnancy ,in which she saw a baby sitting calmly between two big dogs. The baby was dressed as a girl, but with a typical boy's manner and apparent fearlessness. Now my client   understood the message which her spirit baby was giving her in the dream…the baby looked like a girl but was still the little boy she loved!

4.) A client was racked with guilt over having had a termination many years before. She had also had a child whose birthdate was exactly ten years after the termination. Channeling revealed that the date was a very strong message that the Spirit Baby had in fact returned to her mother, and there was no reason for feeling guilt.

5.) Another client had had a series of miscarriages. I determined during Reiki that there was a huge spiritual blockage in her sacral area, and that her miscarriages were not caused by anything physical. We used Reiki and other methods to clear up the spiritual blockage, caused by guilt over something in her past.

6.) Very shortly thereafter , the client told me that counter to all medical predictions, she was again pregnant. When we connected with the Spirit Baby, she presented herself as a little girl of about 2, carrying a basket of flowers. The child, in my mind's eye, gave her mother a daisy, saying "every petal says she loves you." After the session my client said that she had suffered her last miscarriage at home. She could not bear to dispose of the tiny fetus without love, so she buried the products of conception in the garden. Out of that patch of ground had grown a great profusion of daisies. Could the Spirit Baby have been any clearer in her message to her mother that she was now back to stay?

P.S. My client has since delivered her baby- a little boy! I think that Spirit Babies have a sense of humor. Also, at the time the message was sent, the mother had not yet made a baby body, and obviously her baby was not particular about the gender.

CHAPTER TWO: MESSAGES FROM THE OTHER SIDE

The other side includes all those beings who live as close to us as our own heartbeat...only most people are not aware of it, most of the time. The other side thus includes spirits of those who have passed, which fall into several categories.

If they have gone to the light to be healed they will eventually return in some form. For example, in my current work with Spirit Babies, I find that sometimes the deceased parent or grandparent of the Spirit Baby's bereaved mother is there in her aura, helping to care for the Spirit baby.

Spirit babies after a miscarriage are a special case of "passed" beings. Because they have not lived in this lifetime outside the body, they do not have to return to have a life review. So they stay with their mother until they can come back to her...or if not to her directly, then it may be in the form of a relative's child.

Other deceased souls often come back to those they loved in the hope that they will somehow be sensed and able to pass on the message that they are fine.

The other side also includes angels and guides, nature devas, fairies, elementals etc. We all have guides/angels to help us, and it is certainly useful to tap in to all the guidance which is available. We only have to ask.

Most of us have had multiple lives (although there may be some very new souls who have not). I am able to pick up these past lives under various circumstances, for example, when doing a Reiki treatment. Past life imprints are in the person's aura. There may also be deceased loved ones who have messages, and angels/guides, and for most young women and some men, Spirit Babies.

A deceased loved one may choose to become a guide. This is not identical to being an angel although they perform the same functions.

Animals are able to communicate with humans, as every pet lover knows. In fact a beloved and deceased pet may return in another animal body or even to be a pet in another incarnation. I believe the expression "cats have nine lives" actually refers to this. I have been an animal communicator (giving people messages from deceased pets...and communicating with "free" animals who found their way to me when I formed a thought image of them in my mind.) So I believe that animals communicate telepathically by pictures in their minds.

Hence the often-documented phenomenon of an animal knowing exactly when its owner was coming home even if the owner has an irregular schedule. The dog or cat would pick up on the owner's thought pictures of returning home.

I have also been an angel intuitive, which simply means I could tell a client who their angels were, what the names were by which they could be known, and the forms they chose to take in my mind's eye. Clients seemed to find it useful to be more able to communicate with their angels. It's astounding to me that angels appear in so many pictorial forms , and in every religion, and yet some people still think they are totally imaginary.

The single most rewarding work I have done with the other side is my work with Spirit Babies, trying to help them come through to incarnation. They are sometimes called indigo/rainbow/crystal children (or whatever term you want to use)- or newly created souls (or sometimes highly developed old souls) who realize that with climate change and environmental destruction, life on Gaia now will be particularly challenging. Hence they need me to give their parents specific messages before they come in. Dear reader, does this remind you of spiritual experiences you have had? (If you had not had any, you probably would not be reading this).

CHAPTER THREE: THE INFERTILITY AND MISCARRIAGE EPIDEMIC...WHAT CAN YOU DO ABOUT IT ?

I was one of the 40 % of mothers who miscarry a child (my first). A generation later, my son and his wife became one of the one in six couples who were unable to conceive a child within a year. These two events have a lot to do with why my healing practice focusses on these areas.

The rates of infertility (defined as inability to conceive, plus repeated miscarriage) have risen from 6% a generation ago to 17% now. I am not sure why this is not front-page news.

The first thing to acknowledge, if you have had a miscarriage, is that usually you will be able to have a healthy baby afterwards. However, you have to allow yourself time for grieving. It is essential that you have a support group. Official support groups exist in many areas where, bereaved parents can discuss their losses with caring strangers who soon become friends.

In Ontario, where I live, the Perinatal and Infant Loss Network (PAIL) serves this function. I have been a volunteer phone counselor for this organization, for women who are not yet ready to come to a group meeting. If you have had this experience you could talk to your doctor or faith leader, look in community listings for bereavement groups, or share with a close friend, your husband, sister, mother…just don't keep it inside.

Then , for the infertile and for those who have lost a pregnancy, be aware that there are many correctible factors, stress for example. When your body is so stressed that it is in fight or flight mode, the very first thing to shut down is reproduction. Your hypothalamus, which controls both ovulation and implantation, effectively turns both of these switches to the "off" position.

One surprisingly simple solution is Hypnosis for Fertility. All the negative messages which may have been given to you by your doctors-or even by childhood or in-utero messages- can be over-ridden by a few sessions with a hypnotist trained in this modality.

It is possible to regress a client to the in–utero period and have her hear the exact words her mother was thinking. One client I regressed to determine the reason for her fear about trying new ventures heard a voice saying over and over, "my son is dying, my son is dying." I asked her when she came out of trance what she thought that was all about. My client said that when her mother was carrying her, her older brother, (who she never met), was dying of leukemia .It had only been mentioned to her in passing .Yet this message of hopelessness stayed with my client well into her adult life.

All the eggs a women will have in her life are already in place when she is a six-month fetus. So maternal grandmothers are carrying a part of their future grandchildren! And it is important to realize that there is an effect when the original pregnancy was traumatic in any way .

In Hypnosis for Fertility the client is helped to enter a relaxed state , in which the stress of believing one is infertile can be overcome, allowing the body to do its own healing work.

A few sessions of hypnosis can double the success rate of allopathic remedies such as IVF. Or the Hypnosis and Reiki can be used on their own.

A Reiki Master (energy worker)can help you with healing the grief in your womb, and make your womb warm again.

Don't underestimate the need to have excellent nutrition prior to conception. The genetically modified corn which comprises 40% of all processed foods(in the form of high fructose corn syrup and many other ingredients with complex names) wreaks havoc with the reproductive system. In animal studies GM corn was associated with birth defects and miscarriage at very low concentrations. Please don`t microwave your food…it renders it toxic by destroying the individual cells , and destroying 97% of the nutrients in vegetables and fruit.

As an urban farmer I keep bees and chickens, and grow

grapes, cherries and pears. Try to grow at least a few vegetables in your garden or a community garden, or buy organic at least in those cases of fruits or vegetables which are most affected by the toxins in pesticides: apples, celery, strawberries ,peaches, spinach, nectarines, grapes ,sweet bell peppers, potatoes, blueberries, lettuce, kale or collard greens

Generally free of pesticide residue are onions .pineapples, avocado, asparagus, sweet peas, mangoes, eggplant, cantaloupe, kiwi, cabbage, watermelon, sweet potatoes, grapefruit, and mushrooms (thanks to the Environmental Working Group for this information.)

When I taught Holistic Nutrition at George Brown College I always recommended The Omnivore's Dilemma by Michael Pollan and Harvest For Hope by Jane Goodall (the scientist who studied great apes). Another good recent publication is Wheat Belly by Dr. William Davis. Many people nowadays have gluten intolerances which they may not even be aware of. If you are often unwell, or have stomach issues, it is worthwhile checking out the possibility and modifying your diet if necessary.

I also recommend that all prospective parents read The Wise Woman's Guide to the Pregnancy Year by Susun Weed. She is the best living herbalist IMHO, with a multitude of suggestions for preparing for natural pregnancy prior to the conception, through diet and supplements, etc.

Some ideas: Drink raspberry tea daily to strengthen your uterus.

Get carotene daily (carrot juice is an easy source), as carotene is the most highly concentrated in the female body at the site where ovulation takes place.

Cranberry and lemon are helpful in stimulating normal ovulation also.

In addition, you could make yourself an Aromatherapy blend. (I took a two year course in Aromatherapy from Sheridan College).

Essential oils are highly concentrated plant products which have been used for thousands of years for healing. Get clary sage(especially good for women's issues). rose(helpful for the grieving which you may still be doing if you have had a miscarriage or termination), and chamomile(soothing for the body and the soul.) Use three drops of each essential oil in a short glass (one ounce). Sniff it to see if you like the scent; you can always add a drop or two of any of them. Now add an ounce of a carrier oil such as grape seed(the lightest oil)or almond oil(very nice for massage). Have your partner massage it into your abdomen. Within 20 minutes it will enter

the bloodstream and   start to heal your reproductive system.
(If essential oils are not needed by your system the body just
excretes them.)

I would also suggest that you try lucid dreaming (plan to wake
during your dream, become aware that you are dreaming ,
but not wake up. Next change the course of your dream, for
example, by flying in your dream. Third, plan to meet your
baby in your dreamtime. (When I was very pregnant with my
older son I had a dream of a little boy running toward me in a
field of flowers.)

Many parents also feel that meditation helps. Walter Makichen
in his book Spirit Babies says that doing particular chants
helps. Talking to your child (in your mind is fine) helps.
Singing to your child helps (better do that out loud)!.

You see, your baby is trying to reach you already, but as in any
conversation there must be reciprocity that indicates your
willingness to participate. I know it might feel strange at first,
but think of it this way, Most parents are willing to talk to,
sing to, even read to the baby in utero. Be willing to start
before conception ! The little one is already in your aura and
fully aware of all you do and feel.

Clients have reported that when they started doing this they got obvious signs back, such as seeing a butterfly in an unlikely place. The butterfly is a universal sign of transformation. It is also often the form a spirit takes between human lives. One client reported seeing a butterfly in her backyard while texting her husband. At the very same time, her husband was observing a butterfly miles out to sea where he was fishing with his father-in-law.

Just be aware of the fact that your baby wishes to make herself known. Another client has heard her baby calling to her "mommy, mommy mommy " , four times so far. She is not yet pregnant.

Spirit may use a song on the radio or a sign flashing by you as you drive to give a message, although I have not yet heard of a Spirit Baby doing this.

But you can develop your own abilities of –

clairvoyance (seeing things in your mind's eye)

clairaudience(hearing something your baby says)

clairsentience(feeling her presence) or

clair cognizance (knowing something about her without knowing how you know)

if you are motivated and open to the possibility. There will be
many further discussions of these abilities in this book.

Once they understand how it works, almost all mothers (and
some fathers) are able to communicate with their future
babies. In the altered state of consciousness called trance,
virtually all can do so.

CHAPTER FOUR: SPIRITUAL RELATIONSHIPS AND SPIRIT BABIES

All relationships are spiritual! That is to say, their ultimate purpose is to help us develop our spiritual understanding and gradually develop such traits as compassion, kindness, forgiveness, generosity, aesthetic ability (both as artist and audience), family love, the capacity for true friendship, the willingness to sacrifice, idealism, hard work, a willingness not to judge others, and so on.

You may have heard the expression that someone can enter our life for a reason, or a season, or a lifetime. True on all counts. The secretary who talked her boss into hiring the scared young immigrant...became his wife, and they are very happy together.

Another example... a young man had always wanted to travel from Canada to the Czech republic for some unknown reason. When he got to a particular small village, he decided to stay...and met his future wife within two weeks. Why? Because he just knew...his soul mates were calling him.

You may also have heard, "You can pick your friends, but not your family." Ah, now that is completely wrong!

Spirit Babies (The spirits of future babies) *always* pick their parents, and in many cases their siblings too. We all make contracts before we enter each lifetime. So it can also be a mutual choice made before birth to reconnect with someone from another life and complete unfinished business. The members of your biological family-at least some of them-are usually part of your soul family, which may comprise 40-60 people. If you live long enough, you will meet many or most of your soul family.

These are people with whom you have chosen to incarnate, over and over in many different types of relationships, as siblings, parent-child, lovers, friends, teacher-student. The roles change as both parties find different ways to express their love for each other.

They also help each other work out the issues, and develop the character traits, which they have chosen to work on in their before-life contracts on the other side. (I knew when I was five years old that I had come to this life to learn patience. I am still working on it.)To facilitate continuous learning, a mother may become a daughter, a brother may become a friend, a wife may become a sister.

A major problem with Western culture is the over-riding concern with looking for one romantic partner who will ostensibly be the be-all and end-all of life. This simply does not work for many people, if not most. We are meant to experience love on many levels, in many ways. We need to accept that some of these relationships may have nothing at all to do with romance, and many of them may not last for long. It is important to live in the now, since it really is the only place we can live.

How can knowledge about past lives help us?

Well, it's helpful to understand that we choose our life tasks, and the family which will help us develop the character traits we want. Some souls may even choose the hardship of unloving or immature parents, or a disability.

A Spirit Baby has to accept a body with a health issue before birth, or the attachment is simply not made. So it is not completely true that fetuses with defects miscarry naturally. For a miscarriage to happen, it is *also* necessary that the Spirit Baby waiting in line will not accept that disability. Otherwise no babies who were not perfect would ever be born.

The energy of someone in your soul family will draw you to them, even across centuries and continents.

But it is not always perceived as a completely positive experience!

In our time of massive spiritual changes, souls may deliberately choose to have the one they love be in a body of the same gender, or a different religion, or a different nationality.

So many versions of the Romeo and Juliet story abound in every culture because, quite simply, the urge to be with the beloved is strong enough to risk death.   (For example, the Cinderella story of a very poor and mistreated girl attracting a wealthy and powerful man exists in every culture, from Native North American to ancient Chinese).

The barriers to love, which are random and artificial divisions between "us" and" them", are falling now. This is hugely important in the coming together of humanity as One.

Over and over throughout history lovers on The Other Side, when planning their life tasks, have *chosen* to be born to different social classes, races, religions, countries. They have chosen to create barriers in order to be part of the solution-and beat those walls down.

What are some other goals of spiritual relationships?

A friendship serves to let each member of the pair be heard, understood and loved. A friendship group, based on everything from a school class, to an athletic team, to a church choir, serves to create a sense of community.

A parent-child relationship begins, ideally, as a mentoring relationship which encourages the young person to fulfill their potential and complete their life task, but it gradually changes to a friendship between equals, and there may even be role reversal at the end of the parent's life.

Often children have something important to teach their parents. Until   the message is understood, the Spirit Babies may delay their coming in. I guess some people might be startled to get advice from their Spirit Baby! Your child may be as old a spirit as you, or older. Some children come to teach their parents (and ALL children help their parents learn the true nature of adulthood!)

CHAPTER FIVE : HOW I COMMUNICATE WITH YOUR SPIRIT BABY

Years before I had my children I knew I would have two boys, then a girl. I did not understand then that I must have been aware of the Spirit babies lined up in my own aura.

About a decade ago when doing Reiki treatments, I would get messages from Spirit Babies in the mother's aura. I was also able to communicate with my grand-daughter for years before her conception.

I also knew that my daughter had a Spirit Baby in her aura for years. She has now had her little boy.

When I see clients in person it is easy to get in touch with the Spirit Baby, who is always in the mother's aura.

But most of my clients are by email.

I would like to explain how my gift works, as far as possible.

I know it's highly unusual, and I don't control how it comes to me.

It is very hard work and I love it. It takes me at least two hours per session, sometimes three or more.

You see, it requires a particular type of focus, very similar to that of an artist. Now, some artists use sculpture and some use oil paint. Some musicians use drums and some use harps.

My clients say it is very useful, comforting and even amazing to hear what their babies have to say.

I can tune into your energy and that of the other people I ask about with the information (names, birthdates etc.) which I ask client to send me . .

When I see people in person I can hear the messages from their babies **(clairaudience)**.

Sometimes I get a third-eye visual of how the baby is choosing to look at that moment, for example. a two year old girl carrying a basket of flowers**(clairvoyance)**.

If the information is very powerful I get a physical reaction , like a shiver up my spine**(clairsentience)**

Sometimes a great deal of information comes in at once and I just know what needs to be communicated (**claircognizance**.)

Seeing the information of names and birth dates on the page helps me to tune in to the Akashic records of the lives of the spirits involved. I usually work in the wee hours of the morning, when other people's energy is least likely to interfere.

The conversations with spirit babies, grandparent spirits who are often watching the babies etc. are transcribed and sent to you. This is about what the babies wish to say, things they need you to know. They may well choose to address messages to you directly, calling you Mom or Dad.

You are free to add questions to the information you send me and the babies or other spirits (such as guides or spirits of deceased relatives) will answer.

The babies often speak at   a spiritual (adult) level, since they have had previous lives and may present with adult sensibility. The email format is the most effective way to retain the entire message. . Afterwards you can send questions to clarify anything you did not understand.

CHAPTER SIX: DO SPIRIT BABIES HAVE A PREDETERMINED GENDER?

In my work helping parents communicate with their unborn or not yet conceived children I am often asked this I am often asked this question.

This excerpt from a reading will shed some light on this subject.

Christine: (addressing client's deceased maternal grandfather) are you here?

G: I'm here.

Christine: What would you like to say?

G: I had the honor of being my grand-daughter's Spirit Guide all these years.

Christine: What does that involve?

G: Oh, you know, steering her in the right direction. Helping her make correct choices. And reminding her to have fun too. Life is meant to be enjoyed. It can't all be work (smiles).

C: How has she done so far?

G I am very proud of my grand-daughter. She is an adorable, loving person. She will be a great mom. And she chose well. I like her partner. He is a fine young man, responsible, good to her. He will make a good dad.

Christine: They will be wanting to know about the Spirit Baby.

G (chuckles) Well then , I guess I will have to tell them. I hope they are prepared to give me a new lease on life.

C: What do you mean?

G: I would like to come in as one of their children. There is also a little girl here wanting to come in. So we have to discuss who will be first.

Christine: I thought that was usually decided in advance? That one Spirit Baby lined up first?

G: Usually if a Spirit Baby lines up in the mother's aura, which can happen very soon after the mother's birth, that would be the first baby she would have. But I did not do that. I wanted to stay with my grand-daughter as her Guide from the time I crossed over. Now I would like to come back to incarnation as a baby.

Christine: I imagine that her grandma would be intrigued by that!

G: Yes, she is a wonderful woman, and will make a great great - grandma too (chuckles again.) I have missed her, but at the same time I have always been close by. It is possible for Spirit to be in two places at once. I hope that my beloved wife has felt my presence sometimes. It was hard to leave so early. But I was thrilled to have such an important way to stay close to my family.

Christine: So you and the little girl are deciding who will come first?

G: Well, actually we have sort of worked it out already.

Christine : Who comes first?

G: Spirit Babies have no control over the gender of the body which will become available first. It could be a boy or a girl. So if one Spirit Baby is first in line, that baby has to decide whether they want to take the body on offer, so to speak. Some babies just want the parents, regardless of the body's gender. Some have a strong preference as to whether they want to be male or female in this lifetime.

My grand-daughter will be pregnant within a year. But we don't know whether the first baby body will be a boy or a girl. We have both decided though which we want to be. So if a boy is conceived first it will be me who attaches myself to the body.

If it's a girl body, then the girl spirit comes in first.

Christine: How does that work?

G: When the parents make love they form a beautiful gold conception cradle above the mother's head, at her crown chakra. The body of the baby is like a car without a driver before that happens. The Spirit Baby who has chosen the parents goes in to the conception cradle and attaches itself to the body of the baby. That way the baby body becomes viable. Until that happens it's just a body.

Christine : So there are two of you waiting to come in, and you want to be a boy again, while the other spirit baby wants to be a girl.

G: Yes.

Christine: May I speak to the girl Spirit Baby, please?

SB: (peeks out shyly from behind G. G appears to me clairvoyantly in the form of an older man with smile lines around his eyes. The little girl looks about 5. She has the appearance of a Chinese child, which would be her last incarnation.) I need a mommy who will love me.

Christine: I am sure that she will love you.

SB: My last mommy did not want me because I was a girl. She only wanted a boy.

Christine: I understand that this is the law in China, a family can only have one child.

SB: Yes. but I was the first one. I chose that mummy and knew that maybe she would not accept me. Still it hurt very much that she did not want me.

Christine: So your last parents chose not to have you?

SB (looks much younger now, sucking her thumb, speaks in

a small voice) They sent me away before I could be born. It made me very sad.

Christine: Yes, of course it did. I am sure that your new parents will welcome you.

SB: I really wanted to be a girl before. Now I just want a mommy who will really love me even if I am a girl.

Christine: I understand that you want to be loved. I am sure that your new parents will feel that way. I don't think they would love a girl less than a boy.

SB: My big brother is very good to me. He was already here when I came. I was just looking for a mommy and daddy who would not send me away no matter what.

Christine: I think your new mommy and daddy have room in their hearts for two or even more children.

SB: My brother will come in first if there is a boy body, I will come in first if there is a girl body. But what if there are two girls or two boys?

Christine: I guess you and your brother have to talk about

whether you are willing to be either.

SB: I love this mommy and daddy. Mommy is so sweet and kind. I need a mommy like that. I would be willing to be a boy if there are two boys.

G (chuckles) Well, I guess I never thought this through. I have rarely had a life as a girl, but I am positive about the parents I want to be with. And it is possible there could be two girl bodies ,of course. So if I need a lot of extra help in knowing how to become a good woman , my parents will understand why.

Christine: Could you explain?

G: A soul is neither male nor female. Most souls have taken on both genders in different lives for various reasons. The world has changed a great deal even in the time I have been on the other side. And roles are changing so much. In some countries women still are very badly treated as my future sister was the last time. For that reason alone it might be harder to be a woman, if one has rarely experienced those kinds of challenges.

Christine: I guess with gender roles changing so much there

are great challenges in being a woman because there are more choices. At the same time men have to be more involved with their families if they want their wives to be happy.

G: So you are saying that even being a boy will be more complicated than the last time for me?

SB: I have never been a boy, but I am willing to be a boy if there are two boy babies. I just want this mommy and daddy.

Christine: You would have a completely different set of challenges, wouldn't you?

SB: Yes, different things would be expected of me. And I would want to know how to treat a woman properly. That is very important.

Christine: Your parents will be able to help both of you, no matter how it turns out. They love and respect each other and they live in a society where those awful things, like what happened to you, are very unlikely to occur.

SB: But Mommy and Daddy would love a girl just as much as a boy?

Christine: I am sure that your mom and dad, and your other relatives, will love both of you, whether you are boys or girls or one of each.

SB: That makes me feel very happy. I want to be wanted this time.

Christine: I am sure that you will be.
Do either of you have any idea of what your life task and challenges will be?

SB: (clairvoyantly she looks about 12 years old now, and very serious)I want to work in changing the way people think about each other. The way of thinking that made it possible for my parents to discard me because I was a girl. Perhaps as a lawyer, perhaps as a human rights activist, maybe travelling to other countries in the Peace Corps, maybe in some group that works with abused women and children. I want to help make the world a better place for everyone.

Christine: Do you have any ideas about your goal, G?

G: I have enjoyed being a Spirit Guide very much. I think I would like to do some kind of work that involves one-on-one coaching, or teaching, being a mentor with kids. Maybe in the sports field, maybe a child psychologist, I don't know yet. But definitely helping kids find out what they are good at and encouraging them to become their own best selves.

I want to thank my grand-daughter for the wonderful experience I have had being her Spirit Guide(smiles).I like to think I was still just being her grandpa, though on the other side.

Christine: I imagine that your grand-daughter will be happy to hear that she actually had her grandpa with her all along. What will you both need from your parents?

G: I think what every kid needs-an understanding that every child has his or her own hopes and dreams, even before entering this plane.

SB: Mommy and Daddy, we will come to you with past experiences which have shaped us, for good and bad, and we need your help in being the best people we can be.

G: That means, I guess, taking time to play with us, listen to us, understand what a great blessing and responsibility you will be taking on. I don't think I fully understood, the last time around, that there is nothing more important you will ever do *than be a good parent.*

Christine: I am sure that you were a good parent.

G : Sure, I was, most of the time, but to take the time to play with a child, to know that they grow up in the blink of an eye- that's something I would like to instill in my grand-daughter while I am still her spirit guide.

Christine: Who will your grand-daughter's spirit guide be when you become her child?

G (smiles)There is an angel waiting in the wings. She is lovely and gentle. She is here, actually, and she will be with my grand-daughter as her angel soon.

Christine: I understand that children have angels with them from the time of their birth.

G: Yes, and their mother always has access to the guardian angels. So when my grand-daughter becomes a mom she can always call on her children's guardian angels to help with anything that comes up which she needs help with. In fact it is the angels and guides which help mothers have women's intuition.

SB : We would like to come to visit our Mommy in her dreams, and our Daddy too, if he wants.

Christine: What can they do to help that happen?

G: Most people are able to astral travel in their sleep. That just means the sleeping spirit can travel to the other side, where those who have crossed over are, and also the unborn.

Christine: How will they know it's you?

SB : We can take the form of children in our parents' dreams.

G: We can also try to take the form of butterflies in the daytime. It is a form often taken by spirits between lives. Or sometimes a ladybug, dragonfly or unusual bird, such as you would not expect to see in your area.

Christine: So, something with wings?

SB: Yes. But not a bat.(smiles)

Christine: Are you feeling better now, SB?

Spirit Baby: If my Mommy and Daddy love me, that is all I could want.

CHAPTER SEVEN: KARMA, REINCARNATION AND POPULAR CULTURE

Many people have erroneous ideas about the meaning of karma as it relates to past lives. When they are considering having a past life hypnotic regression (under hypnosis) or a past life reading (channeled by another), they express fear that they may have done something bad in a past life and will therefore be punished.

Karma is not about punishment at all. It is more like this basic law of physics: for every action there will be an equal and opposite reaction. This theme is explored in Bruce Cockburn's song Call me Rose.

"*My name was Richard Nixon only now I'm a girl*
you wouldn't know it but I used to be the king of the world
compared to last time I look like I've hit the skids
living in the project with my two little kids
it's not what I would of chose
now you have to call me Rose

I was boss of bosses the last time around
I lived by cunning and ambition unbound...
I was an arrogant man

but now I've got it in hand...

I'm back here learning what it is to be poor
to have no power but the strength to endure
I'll perform my penance well. ".

It is true that "baggage" which has not been cleared up...,such as lack of forgiveness or compassion, can impact negatively on a soul.

A woman who had been a prostitute since age 14 came for a Hypnotic Past Life Regression session to try to change her life for the sake of her daughter. She had a terrible energy at the start of the session, tough and hard and even frightening.

In the first life she regressed to, she was sitting in a prison cell, condemned to death for the killing of her husband (after she found him with another woman). The incarnation of that time described being angry and feeling no remorse for the murder, thinking he had deserved it.(Crimes of passion go unpunished in many countries when committed by men.)

In another life which my client revisited, she was a young man on a platform above a waiting crowd, about to be tortured to death. In this instance the soul had been completely innocent of any wrongdoing, and the fury being experienced was far more extreme.

 In both cases the solution was for the hypnotic subject to be advised to "forgive all wrongs, all pain caused knowingly or unknowingly . let them go ."

By this means she was able to cut all ties with the particular souls who did her harm, *and to let go of the pattern of being the angry victim.*

After the session the client's energy was completely different, normal in fact, so that one would not notice anything unusual about her. *She would no longer attract negative energy to herself.*

Popular culture has recently explored the idea of reincarnation. Cloud Atlas is a movie which explores the journey of a particular soul through male, female and cloned bodies, from centuries ago to centuries in the future .

Common phobias can also originate in a past life. A woman who learned during a regression that she fell off a ship's deck and drowned (in a previous life as a sailor) came to understand her fear of water, and was able to let go of it.

In a more complex situation, a woman came for a regression *specifically because she had suddenly developed a fear of highway driving and suspected a past life reason.*

In her past life the client described being a male, wearing big baggy bloomers and stockings, sitting on the outside seat at the front of a horse-drawn carriage with paying passengers, So the person had been a stagecoach driver, probably in England in the 1700's or 1800's. The client's previous incarnation described driving the coach under a bridge, having a man all in black jump on him and kill him,

He had been killed by a highwayman, and when the client (female in this lifetime) reached the same age, her astral body memory recalled being killed on the highway and so developed a sudden phobia of highway driving.

Understanding this-and doing the forgiveness work-completely cleared up the fear.

On a more positive note, when I was a young college student I started making kaftans for my friends (without a pattern) , and embroidering them. Later I channeled a past life in which I had been a seamstress and embroiderer for the clergy of the Church in England in the late 1600's, making their vestments. The memory of how to do this had spontaneously come back when I reached the same age in this lifetime.

A client came for a Reiki treatment because of debilitating pain which made him unable to work. In his aura I sensed the traces of two past lives-one as an Innuit stone carver and another as a Chinese calligrapher. His body had been in pain because he had given up his dream of being an artist to please his parents, who wanted him to be an engineer. When he understood the message and started to paint, he did not need his pain anymore.

Having another person channel one's past lives is helpful for those clients who are not comfortable with the idea of being hypnotized (due to too many stage hypnosis shows in which they have seen people cluck like chickens). In reality of course therapeutic hypnosis has nothing in common with situations in which volunteers who always wanted to be the class clown get their chance to be amusing.

But in any case, whether one wants to actually relive the

past lives, or to be told about them and their relevance to current issues, makes no difference to the efficacy of the session. In the case of a channeling I require the name and birthdate of the client and those with whom she is having issues at this time .I am able to do this by email. Time and space have no meaning in the spiritual world.

Themes recur over and over in the lives of particular souls until they work them through, have a breakthrough or " aha" moment, and then move onto a higher plane of consciousness.

Souls are male and female in different lives, and also choose to play different roles with others in their soul groups. Two souls may be brother and sister in one life, in another life husband and wife, and in a third lifetime platonic friends.

Souls choose between lives, with the help of their guides, what lessons they need to learn in the next life. They are given choices, but may be gently nudged in the direction they need to go.

Many Spirit Babies (the unborn, not yet conceived souls) find it hard to   return to a life of pain and sorrow (and inevitable death) after experiencing the realms of light and love. They an change their minds at any time up to the point of birth.

This may lead to a stillbirth of an apparently healthy child .

Singer George Harrison wrote the Art of Dying. He followed Eastern religion and philosophies. One of those was reincarnation, which is described in the song's lyrics.

"There'll come a time when most of us return here
Brought back by our desire to be
A perfect entity
Living through a million years of crying
Until you've realized the art of dying
Do you believe me?"

Another song which deals with this theme is "Reincarnation Song" by Toad the Wet Sprocket.

"I thought this light would comfort me
I thought it would be easy
But there's a tugging at my sleeve
And too much baggage I brought with me to leave

Something so big I can't understand
From trying to I would go mad
So I hurry back to little Earth

For another life another birth
Another life another birth .
Mother? "

CHAPTER EIGHT:WOMEN'S INTUITION AND SPIRITUALITY

The freezing rain caused power outages, broken trees all over the roads, and outside it was just at the freezing point. By the time it got down to 14 degrees in the house, only the room with the fireplace was habitable, and my two-month old grandson was bundled up in his snowsuit. My daughter and the baby's father live with me, so I have been very involved in feeding, changing and generally loving the little guy. I advised them to go rent a hotel room for the night while I stayed and took care of the cats and chickens. The hotel they chose was about a 20 minute drive away.

At four in the morning I heard my grandson crying . I thought, "That's odd, why would they have come home in the middle of the night?" When they returned my daughter confirmed that the baby had awakened for his feeding at four in the morning.

This energy connection might not have seemed quite as remarkable if it had been the baby's mother who sensed her child was in need many miles away. We all know that in a playground with a hundred children, a listening mother will hear when her own child is hurt. But my feeling is that such an energy connection can theoretically occur between any two people who care about each other.

I heard from a young man that when he was out hiking in the mountains his mother awakened his father to say, "Joe's in trouble." Then she said minutes later ,"He's all right now."

Joe had stopped in pitch dark to camp, with his sleeping bag (though he did not know it) right at the edge of a cliff. Something made him awaken in the middle of the night, rummage for his flashlight, and then hurriedly find a safer place to sleep.

It is essential for the baby's survival-and this is true in many species-that the mother be tuned in at all times to her young one's safety.

But surely intuition is not limited to mother-child relationships? And why do we speak as if only women have it?

An acquaintance, Vicky, who is an identical twin, said she could always feel what her twin was experiencing. Once when her twin was in a car accident, Vicky experienced the exact sensations her twin was going through.

Vicky had already decided she did not want to have children, but she knew that her sister was planning on having them. So she shut down her intuitive ability for several years because "I did not want to go through labor."

One may have all sorts of explanations as to why an identical twin might be so "tuned in" to her twin that it could become painful. I feel it has to do with the choice Spirit Babies make to become identical twins-arguably the closest relationship anyone could have to another- a choice made before birth and based in previous lives together.

We all know of long- married couples who finish each other's sentences. The implication is that they can read each other's thoughts. Is this just long familiarity-or are they really on the same wavelength in some mysterious way, that involves vibrating at the same frequency perhaps? And is this skill something which all of us could learn-if we only wanted it, and thought it was possible?

What makes these examples of communication across distance-or apparent mind-reading- so compelling is the mysterious energy connection which seems to transcend ordinary boundaries of time and space.

I believe that by definition love is not limited in time, space, or bodily identity.

My mother told me that shortly after my father's death he came to visit her in the night, sat on the bed and said only, "Don't be afraid." She took this to mean that she should not remarry, as he would be waiting for her on the other side. But perhaps he only wanted to say that death is an illusion- that the soul goes on after the body's passing.

It has been scientifically demonstrated that a group of heart patients who were prayed for had better outcomes than another group who were not prayed for. Setting aside for a moment the belief in a higher power mediating the results-is it possible that the focused intention of good towards a person one does not even see or touch can have a profound effect?

And if so, why?

I believe that we create our own reality. If we believe something is possible, we can bring it about. Girls have observed since earliest childhood that their mothers, aunts, grandmothers, and female neighbors know how to soothe their children's hurts, understand what their child needs, and "feel" whether their child is getting into trouble at that very moment.

Yet surely men have those capacities too? Souls are neither male nor female-so if a soul incarnates as a male, does this mean an automatic disadvantage in intuition?

Perhaps- if the message constantly given in the surrounding culture is," That's not appropriate behavior for a male." Even in relatively enlightened societies, there is still quite a lot of sexual stereotyping around gender roles.

My friend was telling me about her friend Peter. He is a house-husband with a small part-time business which does not earn much money. Peter cares for the four children, cooks, and is an excellent listener and nurturer when his high-powered and high-earning wife needs a crying shoulder. But his own self concept is that he is not worth much because he does not make much money!

Peter is a wonderful, nurturing father, which includes being tuned in to his children's feelings. But his wife does not think it is a big deal that he does all the things which traditionally, women in relationships do-keeping up social contacts, creating a home. So a man like Peter is at a tremendous disadvantage in developing skills like intuition, because he does not see that anyone values those skills- or him.

But isn't that what this world needs more of? Shouldn't we be raising our children to be free to be whoever they need to be…with a work-life balance which works for them and their relationships?

Intuitive skills are not limited to direct connections with other human beings, of course.

They can also relate to works of art or scientific discoveries. There is the story about Newton "discovering" the theory of gravity when an apple fell on his head.

Handel's Messiah was written in a period of six weeks in which the composer was in such a trance state that his servants kept preparing food for him but he did not take any time to eat.

JK Rowling , one of the world's most successful authors, told an interviewer that the entire Harry Potter series of 9 books downloaded itself into her brain in a single session while she, as an impoverished single mom and struggling writer, was riding the London Underground. Stephen King also has stated that he writes in a trance state.

These creative activities may also be examples of human beings finding a way to tap into something much larger than themselves -the Field which connects all of us, the Field which ultimately makes us part of one much larger pattern.

It is as if most of the time most people only have cable reception and are content with it, while in fact anyone could have a satellite dish-if they wanted it, and were aware that it was possible to get much more.

In theory, anyone can develop intuitive knowing. When children are born they are full of potential, and they remember things. As William Blake says, we come "trailing clouds of glory."

One little girl of four told me,   " I have something to tell you. Before when I was big and my daddy was little, he was my baby and he was in my tummy."

Another   child of two said, "Can you help me do up my buttons? Before when I was huge I could do it but now my little hands don't remember how."

In western culture such knowing is usually attributed to imagination. Yet what is a child prodigy-like Mozart , who wrote "Twinkle Twinkle Little Star" at the age of 5-but a child who has not yet forgotten what he once knew?

Spirit speaks to us all the time. If we ask a question of the universe, the answers will come in an amazing number of ways. We can develop (or just allow) clairaudience (hearing) clairsentience (gut feeling) claircognizance (knowing without having been taught), or clairvoyance(seeing or understanding with an inner eye.)

So a mother hoping to conceive may hear a child 's voice saying "Mommy mommy mommy" when there is no child around (clairaudience).

In Japanese folklore the soul between lives takes the form of a butterfly. A woman hoping to conceive may see a butterfly in her garden while her husband (who she is texting) sees one miles out to sea. This is clairvoyance.

Meaningful coincidence is one way that Spirit speaks. Many, many women have felt the soul of their child alight inside them(clairsentience) or just knew that they were pregnant before tests confirmed it (claircognizance.)

As fathers take a more and more active role in caring for their young children-starting with the Lamaze classes and attending births, continuing with the diaper changing and all the other nitty –gritty of caring for very young children ,there may be a really major change in perception. We may find that we learn to understand what intuition really is. Intuition is a very great gift which we all have, and we all can develop… connection to each other and to All That Is.

CHAPTER NINE : DEALING WITH THE LOSS OF AN UNBORN CHILD

Conduct a Ceremony for the loss of an unborn child

What if you have some issues to resolve with your Spirit Baby?

Many parents have lost children through miscarriage or other causes. If it was a termination, (and even with miscarriage) there is often guilt. Parents should realize that the spirit of their child does not feel anger.

They may say," Mommy, I know that was not the right daddy for me."

They always want to know, "Do you want me now?"

Sometimes there was a past life issue involving hurt caused between parent(s) and Spirit Baby, although it may have been inadvertent or involuntary.

This is a little ceremony which honors the past and looks forward to the future.

Invocation:

Light a candle

Call on Mother Mary/Quan Yin/Kali/Pacha Mama/any Divine
Feminine energy you are comfortable with to help

These divine female energies understands all about the
pain of losing a child.

Focus:

Reflect on what your Spirit Baby has told you.

Or focus on your feelings about your (future) child.

And/or focus on the one you have lost and say the words.

" I bless and forgive all who may have hurt me for any pain
caused,

knowingly or unknowingly,

willingly or unwillingly, in any past circumstance.

I also bless and forgive myself for my past failings.

Please bless and forgive me for any harm I may have done you in any past situation.

Please bless and forgive others who have hurt you also."

It helps all the souls move on.

The lingering negative associations   can be broken.

Completion:

Sit quietly until you feel a sense of lightness.

CHAPTER TEN: THE HEALING POWER OF FORGIVENESS

Back Story: a couple is faced with the decision of whether or not to terminate a child with a serious disability

Spirit Baby: Mommy, let me tell you in advance that my identity as a spirit is somewhat different than my expression in one particular body.

Imagine a normal hand-you can imagine it as a child's hand.

On each fingertip is a photo of a human face.

Maybe there are two or three females, at least two races, and one finger with a photo of a disabled child.

The palm of the hand represents the higher self. (This is a simplification, as in fact we may have hundreds of lives.)

(switches apparent age to baby form)Mommy, I want you to hear me...both as a baby in one incarnation, and as a spirit with a great many lives.

(older sounding spirit) Each expression of that higher self is quite different due to heredity, family, gender, social class, *physical health. And these different characteristics radically affect the options which that expression will have in the society into which it is born.*

Parents have the right and duty to prevent suffering in their children. If a disabled child will not fit into your family life, and you feel you would not be able to give him unconditional love, then there is no blame and no shame.

From me, there is no anger, Mother, if this is the difficult choice you have to make. It frees me to go on to have a healthier life at some future time, a little sooner.

As for me, with my consciousness still on the other side, I know that life on Earth is very hard at the best of times. On the Other Side there is only joy and peace and talk of future opportunities to fulfill a life task.

It is true that even a disabled person can have a life task. For example, he or she may help others who are their caregivers develop qualities of compassion, caring, forgiveness, patience, and joy in simple things.

On a soul level, I am your child and will continue to be so even if my physical body is not allowed to continue. If this is the decision you need to make there is no blame, no anger. I would stay on a soul level...at the very least I could be an inner child to you, Mommy, reminding you to take time to smell the roses.

As a child with mental and physical disabilities that might be my own orientation, but it would be harder for you to have that time. Also the care of a disabled child is a lifetime task...which tends to fall on the sibling to carry on with.

*I could certainly detach my spirit from the body before the procedure so that I would not feel any discomfort-more like a car **without a driver** crashing, to use an image you might understand.*

Please be aware that I am speaking from the point of view of my higher self. It does not mean that an expression with mental disabilities could ever think this way.

Mother: I am very sad and very confused as I am not sure this Spirit Baby wants to join us. I feel as if we are doing something wrong.

SB: My love for you makes me willing to take on any challenges...but this does not mean that I expect great sacrifices from you, daddy and big sibling. Life is about making choices which work for all concerned-including me, mother.

You are the best mommy I could ask for, and even now, while I am still in your body I am blessed to feel your emotions. ..your love and concern for me. This experience will help me be a better guide/inner child/secret friend, if that is what remains as options.

I love you all, and as you may be aware, I have no control at all over what bodies are provided...I can only decide whether to attach, for the experience, or not. For me there is no pain, emotional or physical, if the particular expression of my higher self which is a body with huge challenges has a short rather than a long life. It is still an experience, which I thank you for...a learning opportunity to be a part of your family for a while in the physical realm. No life is wasted, mommy.

Mother: I lost a close friend. Is there any message?

Friend: Love is the only thing you can take with you to the other side.

*It is peaceful here. There is time for reflection, but there is
also a lot of work to do.*

We will meet again.

*If you should happen to meet a child or adult, years from
now, who reminds you of me, remember not to be fooled by
gender or race or anything like that. Energy stays though,
energy is the same life after life, when you have really
known and loved someone. A part of me will always be here
on the other side to welcome you home.*

*I know you are going through a very difficult time- I look in on
you sometimes. Try to remember that joy will return. You
have a beautiful child. Your child needs you to take care of
yourself. So rest as much as you can, meditate and realize
that there is a bigger picture which we cannot fathom while
we are still trapped in the very slow, heavy energy of Earth.*

*I am free now from all the pain and suffering. The instant I
left my body the pain was gone-it was quite amazing.
And no, I did not learn all the secrets of the universe at once!
But I realized that there is a far bigger picture than we can
ever grasp while we are still in the Earth body.*

You are very deeply loved.

The Spirit Baby you are carrying has chosen you and will stay with you all your life in some form. You will not lose him -I know that seems hard to understand, but do you think you have truly lost me, your friend? Am I not still a part of you? Any time we love someone truly, they are a part of our souls forever-through future lifetimes to come. Love is the ONLY thing which death does not change -the only thing we can take with us to the other side, and into future lives.

Please believe that sorrow fades. Joy will come in the morning.

CHAPTER ELEVEN: HOW DID THE HUMAN RACE LOSE TOUCH WITH THE SACRED FEMININE?

Hundreds of years ago, in the region of the Great Lakes, the indigenous people were farmers and hunters. The women farmed corn, squash and pumpkins. During the long winters the people were warm and snug in their longhouses, structures which could hold ten families and ten cooking fires, with long shelves in at least two layers all along the walls, one layer for sleeping on, a higher one for storage.

The women grew the food which provided 90% of the calories. The men hunted and protected the group. Older women chose the chief, and if he did not perform his duties well, they chose a new one.

Men and women thus had different functions, but there was mutual respect.

The society changed radically with the coming of the white settlers. The first contact with French voyageurs was for the most part peaceful, with many of the French fur trappers marrying native women.

But the British Hudson's Bay company paid for the furs which wealthy Europeans wanted- in alcohol. The native people did not have any experience with alcohol, nor thousands of years of built-in capacity to tolerate it.

The men quickly became prey to alcoholism. In their new topsy- turvy world a man who showed signs of being inebriated must be a good hunter, for he had obviously traded many valuable furs for his drink!

This illusion became more important than the reality.

For the furs which were wanted were mink and beaver, not the deer and turkey and even rabbit which had provided a stable source of protein for the family. And if a woman complained to her husband that the mink meat was inedible ...the inhibition which alcohol releases might lead to family violence.

Such disrespect for women had never been a part of the culture. The alcohol-and different goals for hunting-quickly changed the culture in negative ways.

Later the Residential Schools in Canada took the children forcibly from their parents and subjected them to physical, emotional and sexual abuse. A high percentage of the children died. Within a few centuries the respect for women and the Divine Feminine (native North American version)was lost.

Scroll back a few more centuries to Medieval Europe. Midwives were in charge of almost all births. Midwives were all women who had given birth, perhaps many times. They also were women who had a natural gift for healing, perhaps with gentle hands and soothing voices. They knew what local plants could staunch bleeding, heal broken bones, soothe the pain of childbirth, and calm childhood fevers.

In a largely illiterate setting in which nothing was understood about germs, women still, for the most part, were able to help other women give birth successfully. All women were expected to keep their homes as clean as possible (the original meaning of slut was a woman who did not keep her house clean). So aside from issues like breech birth(which an experienced midwife could still sometimes deal with) most women survived childbirth.

Those who went to male doctors did not fare as well. A doctor might go from a patient who had an infectious disease directly to the birth without washing his hands (and the mother would die of puerperal fever).

However, the healers aroused the ire of church authorities. When they made healing blends of medicinal herbs they were accused of making magic potions.

The real problem was that they alleviated the pain of childbirth. The church leaders said that according to the Bible, Eve was the cause of original sin, and was punished by the pain of childbirth. So easing that pain was the work of the Devil.

Nine million women were burned as 'witches" in the Burning Times, which lasted centuries in all parts of Europe. Who were they really- now that we know there is no such thing as witches?

They were the most intelligent, compassionate, knowledgeable , and perhaps outspoken women of their time. In other words, a real threat to the authorities. But just being female was enough to put someone under suspicion.

Sometimes a group of Portuguese or French fishermen would go off to sea for a time, leaving their village unprotected. They would come back and find every single female in the village, down to the babies, had been burned at the stake. (Of course the smaller boys would also have died without care.)

Prior to patriarchal religions (Judaism, Christianity, Islam) and patriarchy's view of women as inherently inferior, most people were far more open to the concept of equality between men and women, and the notion of women as exemplars of the Earth Mother Goddess.

In that time, over two millennia ago, the Druids worshipped the Earth Mother in forest groves. The temple priestesses in Egypt were visited by worshippers who wanted to know their futures. The Romans , Greeks and Vikings had a great many gods and goddesses who specialized in all sorts all sorts of tasks ..like Freya, the Viking goddess of springtime and Athena, the Roman goddess of the hunt.

Ceres was a goddess of agriculture, grain crops, fertility and motherly relationships. She was originally the central deity in Rome.

Shakti is the concept, or personification, of divine feminine creative power, sometimes referred to as 'The Great Divine Mother ' in Hinduism. On the earthly plane, Shakti most actively manifests through female embodiment and creativity/fertility, though it is also present in males in its potential, not yet manifest form.[

Long before that, tens of thousands of years ago, small statues of pregnant fertility goddesses showed the veneration of men for the female creative capacity.

We can only assume from the available evidence that women through much of pre-history had a position based on the prevailing wisdom. There were two genders of God and Goddess, and in turn human women also had an importance based on their identification with Mother Earth-as men could identify with Father Sky.

So what went wrong?

Well, one particular group-European males- had the leisure to develop technology. This was due to several accidents of environment -such as the abundance of large trees suitable for ship-building, the availability of animals which could easily be domesticated and plants which could easily be grown for food, and metals such as iron available in abundance for potential forging into weapons and plowshares.

Why would this impact on the males in the environment more than the females?

Basically, when large groups are able to live in one place due to the development of agriculture , this makes way for a leisure class who can devote themselves to such things as inventing things , writing, etc.

In a time before birth control, of course, women of any social class spent much of their time giving birth to, and raising, large families. And men, being in general physically stronger, and also not encumbered by pregnancy and children, were far more likely to go to sea, or war, or develop new inventions, or write about what they experienced life to be. (We all know that male and female writers speak in rather different voices.)

Now, none of this inevitably had to lead to wars of conquest (of all the other continents and races) or a change in women's perceived acceptable roles. Unfortunately power corrupts, and absolute power corrupts absolutely.

European males won the environment   lottery and so were able to forge ahead rather quickly with technological advancement (sailing ships, successful mixed farms, and weapons of war. And don't forget writing-which allows those with an education to set the rules and control the information flow –since knowledge is power too.)

Thus over a period of several centuries, things changed-in some case quickly, in others more slowly. Men were perceived to have the power…so those who wrote the religious texts, the scientific treatises and the stories of epic battles told these things from their point of view. Powerful males were in charge. God must be male (Judaism, Christianity, Islam) .

The gradual implementation of a belief system which put European males at the top of the hierarchy (with God looking like an old white male, and no room at the inn for females in the father, son, holy ghost trinity, for example) also gradually became associated with the subjugation of women and of all other races- to the full extent that European males could accomplish this with their superior technology. (Islam, another patriarchal system, is not known for treating women any better.)

Okay, so what's a person to do?

I am happy to see so many of my sisters and brothers of all ages and colors are doing the difficult work of re-thinking what it means to be human. There is Malala , a teenager who risked death by insisting on education for girls in Pakistan. There is Hilary Clinton, former secretary of state for the US who quietly goes around the world encouraging grass-roots projects to encourage women's rights. There are the millions of dedicated teachers and parents who encourage girls to dream big and boys to express all their emotions . There are the individual women who encourage their men to get fully involved in child-rearing ...and all the men who "get it". There are those who combat spousal abuse, child marriage, the killing of baby girls in India and China, sexual slavery in many countries ...and those brave children who aspire higher than their own parents or societies "allow."

This is the biggest human rights issue in the history of the world.

Women hold up half the sky.

Or to use another image, the bird of humanity cannot fly with only the male or the female wing. Both wings need to be equally strong for humanity to fly to the greatest heights.

CHAPTER TWELVE: WHAT DOES THE SPIRIT BABY SAY?

In the hilarious you-tube viral video "What Does the Fox Say?" by Ylvis, the lead singer bemoans the fact that he is unable to communicate with a fox, which he describes as "*You're my guardian angel, hiding in the woods*". He goes on to say "*if you should meet a friendly horse, would you communicate by Morse*?" The punchline occurs when the fox appears in the background and does a song and dance routine. But the singers in the front of the scene are too busy bemoaning the difficulty of communication to see or hear him, and he vanishes again.

Let's compare this to Spirit Baby communication.

Most mothers do understand that it is possible to communicate with the baby while pregnant. They can observe that the baby responds to the energy of different people who come near the mother, particularly the father, and also responds to the mothers' mood.

Now let's look at the typical Spirit Baby scenario, when the mother is having difficulty either getting pregnant or staying pregnant. She may even have had a termination which she deeply regrets. How can she communicate with the child who is "hiding in the woods", as far as she is concerned?

1.) Clairvoyance(clear seeing)

"I now sing to and talk with my Spirit Baby often often...and I know she hears me. I asked her for an obvious sign, that I needed to know it was her. A feather flew right into my hands the following day.... It wasn't a bird's feather, it wasn't a pillow feather, it was a feather like I have never seen. I knew it was her sign for me. "

This mother is developing her clairvoyance- the ability to "see" the message in something visual which is out of place and directly relates to a spiritual issue.

In another example the Spirit Baby often takes the form of a bird or butterfly.

"Mother: The bird with a beautiful red chest flew into our house 3 days ago
They say it's for death
Your daddy said it's a new life

Was it you?

Your mommy"

Spirit Baby; "Yes, Mommy ,that was me. "

In a third example of clairvoyance ,the mother had learned that in Japanese lore, the spirit between lives takes the form of a butterfly.

She saw a lovely butterfly in her garden, and excitedly texted her husband, who was miles out to sea fishing with his father-in-law. At the same moment, her husband saw a butterfly over the ocean. (Yes, spirit can appear in two places at once.)

2.) Clairaudience(clear hearing)

Another "clair" which can be developed-once the mother realizes it is possible to have communication with the spirit realm –is clairaudience.

When mothers of babies who are not yet conceived hear a small voice (and there is no other child speaking nearby) the voice says very simple words such as "Mommy Mommy Mommy" or "I'm here" .

There may also be the mother's own higher self, clearly audible as her own voice, saying "This is going to work" which was interpreted as meaning , "Spiritual communication is being established and pregnancy will follow."

3.) Clairsentience (clear feeling)

A mother wonders, "When I sing to my Spirit Baby I do not hear a voice. I do not see anything. But I feel all warm and fuzzy inside. Does that mean anything?"

Yes, it does. This mother is feeling clairsentience- a feeling associated with love, with holding a baby .Her own heart energy is making her feel warm and fuzzy when it feels the answering love of the spirit baby in her aura.

4.) Claircognizance (clear knowing)

Finally, there is the phenomenon of Claircognizance

One mother had been traumatized after her miscarriage by a know-it-all doctor who recited all the medical reasons why miscarriages could occur, finishing off with these words, "And some girls (sic) can't have babies at all. They just have miscarriage after miscarriage."

Let's put aside the obvious riposte about demeaning language. The most important things the doctor was missing were 1.) bedside manner and 2.) the awareness that miscarriage is very often a means to an end of spiritual awakening in the mother.

When this mother became pregnant again she worried throughout her pregnancy that it would not last. Finally she asked her child for a sign.

That night she dreamed of a little boy running towards her in a sunlit meadow. She "just knew" that this was a sign from the baby that he was all right. She delivered a healthy boy.

The function of "women's intuition" (which men can also have) is to make a mother aware of her child's needs, especially when there is a problem and the child may not be physically present to her senses. A woman becomes a mother when the spirit baby chooses her, which may be years before she gives birth.

Because of the need to care for and protect her child, all mothers have the potential to develop one or all of the clairs. Some are more comfortable with one or another. It is not necessary to use more than one, once communication has been comfortably established with the spirit baby. When the mother is sure her unconceived child can hear her, it becomes easy to say the only things that really need to be said, "I love you, Daddy loves you , (big brother or sister are looking forward to you, if applicable) and we are ready to have you join our family."

And singing a lullaby seems to soothe every baby-whether before or after birth. Mommy's voice is always the voice of an angel!

P.S. Spirit Babies are capable of extremely detailed and complex communication too, as they may temporarily take on the adult form they may have had in a previous life when they knew the mother. They may tell why they chose their parents, what the karmic connections were, and why they are having difficulty coming in. Generally it requires the help of an experienced medium to get these more complex messages.

CHAPTER THIRTEEN: HELP BRING IN YOUR OWN BABY

I believe that you will develop your own ability to communicate directly with your future baby.

I suspect that you are more intuitive than you know. The things which are most important to you are important to your child also. The values , the goals, the words , the images when you learn to communicate will be similar to yours. After all this is why you made this agreement to share a life together.

Whether your experience starts with a few words remembered from a dream, a flash out of the corner of your eyes, or a feeling of someone else being in the room, it will come. I don't think you will have to wait until you are pregnant to experience it. Your Spirit Baby chose you long ago. You already know each other.

In order to use the Law of Attraction, though, it is not enough to use words and ideas. It is helpful to buy a small item such as booties or a sleeper, just to make it clear to the baby that you are preparing for your future together. Also, journal your thoughts about the baby in a dedicated little notebook daily.

Buy or make a card and write a message to the baby. Use candles when meditating. Light attracts guides , angels and positive spirits.

Physical things associated with the baby make it seem closer to **you**, but you are also showing your preparations to the future baby. Your baby is most likely in your heart chakra, basking in the love energy generated by your heart. You could get a small cloth bag with these small tokens in it, and take ten minutes a day to visualize the baby using all your senses. (You could add baby powder or whatever makes you think of a baby.) Sing to the baby daily.

When you do your daily meditation, imagine the feeling of your baby in your arms. Draw what you think the baby will look like . The more you visualize and creatively imagine , the easier it will be for your body to achieve pregnancy and birth. You are informing your body of your intention to achieve a successful full-term pregnancy. You are also informing the watching baby in your aura that you are preparing for the arrival of your new family member.

It is a form of self-hypnosis, and it does work. Now let's talk about why hypnosis works.

We tend to believe what we are told over and over. Some women may have taken in the message, "You will not be a good mother." Some may believe it because they themselves have experienced abuse. Some people may have repeatedly heard from authority figures, "You are too old to have a baby." Some feel tremendous guilt about a termination years before, or even a miscarriage. Some may think the inability to conceive means they did something wrong although they don't even know what it is.

None of these are helpful beliefs. And they can be overridden rather quickly in hypnosis.

The hypothalamus, just above the brainstem and roughly the size of an almond, controls important aspects of parenting and attachment behaviors, and also both ovulation and implantation. When your body is in fight or flight mode, both of these shut down.

What causes fight or flight mode? Stress. The stress of believing you are infertile is as great as cancer or grief. (Well, of course it is an extreme form of grief.)

But we know that the body heals itself when given rest, proper food, and hope. For a supposedly infertile couple, being accepted for adoption often releases the stress-and results in pregnancy. Hypnosis for fertility is a lot easier than being accepted for adoption.(Spirit babies can choose their adoptive parents, but that is another article.)

The mother is given meditation-type images to help her relax. Then she is gently told" set down the weight of all those burdens you have been carrying. Let Mother Nature wrap her arms around you, or perhaps you would prefer a warm blanket of universal love. Good?

Now, surrounded by love, realize that you can heal yourself. Let go of the I can't s, the I shoulds, the judgements . And know that you can heal yourself and let your abundant life-force energy come to the surface."

Yes, that's about it. Sometimes a few sessions are needed as the resistance peels back like the layers of an onion. But even one session can double the success rate of technological procedures. (Although it is true that Spirit Babies prefer the natural way. But that's another article.)

CHAPTER FOURTEEN: CONNECTING DIRECTLY WITH YOUR SPIRIT BABY IN TRANCE

If you are a woman who has contracted before this lifetime to have a child, you have a Spirit Baby. And if you have a Spirit Baby, you already have women's intuition.

Being able to connect intuitively with your offspring is essential to the survival of babies...since 99.9% of young babies are cared for by women, and 100% of babies are birthed by women. Women's intuition does not develop after giving birth, but rather before even conceiving. The spirit pre-exists the individual lifetime.

Yes, of course men can be intuitive. But since almost all spirit babies are in the mother's aura (although the contract may include a particular father) women do have a distinct advantage in developing this intuition. Hence the term women's intuition.

Intuition means a heightened awareness of the four clairs.

Clairaudience means hearing something which is out of place. Clairvoyance means seeing a message in something which is out of the ordinary in the environment.

A woman and her mother were sharing a hotel room. They were both psychically aware. "Marjorie" had been aware for years of fleeting glimpses of a little girl(not solid-looking), footsteps at night , doors opening and closing at night, a little girl's voice saying "Mommy". On this occasion Marjorie asked her presumed spirit baby to give her a clear message, right then, away from her home.

The bathroom light suddenly went on. When Marjorie and her mother went to investigate, the whole fixture had been pulled out of the wall by an unseen hand.

The messages (implied)? "I am here, I am a light being, I am very powerful, I am actively communicating with you and trying to get your attention. "

Clairsentience means feeling something with the emotions . Claircognizance means "just knowing" without physical evidence that something is true. Which is it when a mother "just knows' or "just feels" that she is going to have a boy or a girl? Probably both.

Anecdotally, this happens a lot more often than chance. Women who have already had one baby are likelier to be able to predict the gender of the one they are now carrying, saying that "the energy just feels different."

Hypnosis for Fertility aims to help a mother release emotional blockages, which may interfere with the capacity to conceive or even to carry a pregnancy. All of us have enormous capacities to heal ourselves of broken bones, illnesses , fatigue…why not infertility?

The emotional and spiritual causes   of fertility issues can go at least as far back as the in-utero stage. 100% of all the eggs a woman will ever have are already in the womb, in embryonic form, by the time the fetus is six months old. Unborn babies are 100% aware of their mother's emotions while carrying them…as can be shown when a client is regressed to in-utero.

I asked a friend to regress me to in-utero, to determine what happened to the spirit of my older brother who passed at one month…I was born nine months later.

It did not surprise me to learn that Eric immediately became my guide; I had always felt an affinity to the brother I had never "met."

So, I wondered , could a mother initiate communication with a Spirit Baby who was in her aura but not yet attached to a body? Worth a try…why not make it part of Hypnosis for Fertility, with a focussed "meeting" with the future child

…mother in trance , questions which were previously decided upon being asked by the therapist? In theory this could happen during pregnancy…but also even before the child was conceived. And yes, hypnosis can be done by phone quite effectively.

Situation One

The mother was not sure that she was with the right man.

"Do you have a message for mommy?"

In her trance state she experienced Clairvoyance.

A little boy came up to mommy and daddy with a big ribbon and tied them together!

"Do you have a message for daddy?'"

Now the little boy went up to daddy and kept poking him, saying, " I'm here daddy, I'm real!"

She thought that was pretty cool.

She said that her partner kept kidding her every time she wanted to talk about her pregnancy

saying "I'll believe it when I see it."

So obviously the baby had been tuning in!

You need to think about what you are actually trying to find out when you compose your questions.

Situation Two

"Do you have a message for mommy?"

(Mother feels warmth…clairsentience… indicates love and presence)

"How do you try to talk to me?"

(Mother sees a light...clairvoyance… message that spirit baby is still a light being)

Situation Three

Question: "What is the purpose to this fertility journey?

(Mother hears words…clairaudience) "Love."

Question: "Is there another spirit with you?"

 "At times"

Question: if so, who?

"Guides"

Question: Is my life task to be a healer?

"Yes"

Question: What am I supposed to be learning?

"To love and be loved."

Do you communicate with your big brother?

"Yes."

Situation Four

Question: How can I make it easier for you to come in?

(Mom gets a clairvoyant picture of a little girl skipping through a garden).

She takes this to mean, have fun in the process.

Question: What do we need to know about the birth?

Clairaudient reply:" It's easy."

Question: Will Mommy be able to have a natural birth?

Clairsentient /clairaudient reply : "Undecided."

Question: Will you come early, late or on time?

Mother hears giggling. Takes this to mean, timing   will be fine.

Question: What will you need to feel at home when you arrive?

Clairvoyant and clairaudient answer: "safety"   and a visual of a blanket which the mother had as a baby.

As a birth shaman, every mother brings the soul of another from the other side to this plane. This is at least as important as bringing the body over .Developing intuitive communication is within   every mother's capacities…and can be a wonderful affirmation of the sacredness of motherhood.

CHAPTER FIFTEEN: MESSAGES FROM YOUR SPIRIT BABY

It is a sad fact that these days many more Mothers and Fathers have a harder time making healthy babies than at any time in the historical past . It is not your fault that this world is so terribly polluted. But you can do your part to help to bring in a healthy child by making some changes to your diet, your supplements, your meditation practice. Most of all, have faith in yourself. To be a good mother to me you will have to inform yourself of all these massive climate changes and other changes in the environment anyway.

You see, there are so many things wrong with the air and the water and the food these days... issues far worse than a lack of food in some other times in the past.

Mothers and Fathers have to be especially careful to eat healthy food, to find time and space to be out in Mother Nature, to be at peace despite the frantic pace of modern life. It is harder now to be a mother than in times past. But it is still the most natural thing in the world, when you give yourself a chance, and let yourself find calm through meditation ... or by learning to communicate with your spirit baby directly, for your Spirit Baby will send you signs like birds and butterflies.

It is not that hard to communicate with a Spirit Baby; most mothers do so unconsciously; it is what women's intuition is all about. Perhaps most important is that you are as calm and peaceful as possible.

Mommy, it is not your fault that your body could not keep the baby body which you and daddy made for me. I will be a healthy baby, when you are able to make me a body to which I will willingly attach. I don't know if it helps you to realise that you will only have a healthy baby in future, because I will not accept a body which is not perfect.

I will be an environmental warrior as my life task. I will do all I can to help Mother Nature in her struggle against pollution, bad air, dirty water, toxic food. The battle to save Mother Nature starts with the youngest and the weakest, which are most vulnerable to toxins. All over the world fish are dying, bird species are dying , and animal species are becoming extinct ... sometimes it is not noticed right away, because the youngest died first , and then there are no adults in a few years to carry on ...

Now Mother, you might find it puzzling that I do not always talk like a baby. I have had many lives, Mother; I have been a diplomat and a faith leader and a homemaker ... because no soul is incarnated in only one gender. And in the past, even the most capable women had few options as to what to do with their lives.

But at this time I am speaking to you in the form of a male, and you will find once you learn to understand my messages, communicate with me ...and you will...that sometimes I will speak as the old soul I am, and sometimes only as the little boy who loves you very dearly.

My life task is to help to clean up the world in which I will live, and to help the many sister and brother species which humans have hurt through environmental degradation and climate change. I am planning to be an earth healer. Like many of the new children, I will come in with a heightened spiritual awareness. And sometimes we even find that our mothers are readier to hear us because, being sensitive, we have had a harder time coming in than they expected. We new children are the tip of the iceberg, the canary in the coal mine.

When people talk of rainbow children, crystal children, indigo children, star children ... these are names for babies who come in with an unusual or deep awareness of the spiritual interconnectedness of life, despite the societies into which we are born, which have often forgotten what was previously always known.

There was a time not so long ago when almost everyone understood this. It was taught within the family and community ... that you must love the Earth as you do your own mother, love the land which feeds you, and the rivers which provide you with clean drinking water. And so when mothers have a hard time bringing healthy babies into the world it very often starts them on a spiritual journey to rediscover the task of all of us... to care for our only home, the Earth.

You and Father are not personally at fault for the issues which have made it harder for people and many animals to carry a healthy baby. But you and Father can make some changes in your life and then I will come to you.

And you will have learned so much about how to live in harmony with other beings that you will be ideally suited to teach me to perform the life task which I have chosen for myself. For you have already started on your spiritual journey. Mommy, I have always been here, I was always in your aura and aware of your love for me and your concern. I love you and I will come in.

Please sing to me. It tells me that you know I am real and always here. It encourages me to come in even though large parts of the world are not half so beautiful as they were centuries ago... The storms were natural, not human-caused; the food was simple, but plentiful and healthful when the rains came, and almost all human babies were born perfect.

Keep letting me know that you love me. Show me by learning more about what I have been talking about, by being willing to give me the kind of home I will need, close to clean water, close to clean air, with space for getting to know animals and plants and waterways in their natural state.

I chose you because of deep love for you and Daddy. We have known each other in many past lives. We always want to come back to those we have loved, but we change the roles to find new and different ways to express the love.

When I see that you have made a healthy baby body, I will be overjoyed to come in through the conception cradle above your head, (when you and daddy have been loving each other) which will be like a beacon welcoming me home.

CHAPTER SIXTEEN: SPIRIT BABIES AND SHAMANISM

Every woman who successfully gives birth is a Birth Shaman. She brings the soul of the child over from the other world which is our real Home...into this world, which is illusory at best, and painful to experience at worst (although at some fleeting moments of full awareness it may well be breathtakingly beautiful.)

Coming into this plane implies a great leap of faith by the Spirit Baby, who leaves the other side (where all is light and love)...They do not always go willingly! The Spirit Baby always chooses parents who will help it learn what it needs to learn in this incarnation. It chooses, not always the most loving and caring of parents, but those who will help it- sometimes by presenting a great challenge. So a child whose life task is to be a musician may choose parents who will encourage and nurture this goal...or parents who make it almost impossible to fulfill because they are impoverished or brutal.

And it is a given that the Spirit Baby chooses , sometimes , a very challenging environment and social circumstances . So for example. Martin Luther King and Nelson Mandela both had to be born black in racist societies to fulfill their life tasks. In both cases, they sought freedom and equality for their own people…yet …it is sad to think how many people do not yet understand that we are all one HUMAN race. (And all Spirit Babies have belonged to different ethnic backgrounds, genders and social classes.)

Being a Shaman means making the Other Side (of peace and love and "magic") evident and present in this reality. So all those who choose to work in order to advance human understanding or a love of beauty , be they Michelangelo the artist or Beethoven the musician or Marie Curie the scientist or Hildegarde von Bingen the visionary , have taken part in the path of the Universal Shaman.

The Spirit Baby who became Martin Luther King may have known before he embarked upon his life task that martyrdom might well await him. The spirit baby who became Anne Frank may have understood too that her life was going to be one of sacrifice. For if she had not been born Jewish shortly before the Holocaust, she would not have written the book which has moved millions, even to tears , just to think that a 15 year old could be killed for her ethnic heritage.

So there is a sense in which anyone who truly becomes aware of, accepts, and embarks upon their life task...despite the obstacles they will inevitably face, the challenges to be overcome...and sometimes the suffering to be borne...is embarking on a shamanic journey of a lifetime's duration .

Spirit Babies, at the time of their birth, are all potential shamans...that is, "they come trailing clouds of glory" as William Blake said. They bring the light of understanding, the understanding which we all entered this world with. And any of them will speak with the wisdom of many lifetimes, to any who choose to hear...a skill which any mother can learn. (Yes, and   some fathers too, although not as many seem open to the possibility.)

All this does NOT mean that if a child does not come to birth the mother has failed in her task of Birth Shaman. For often it is not until decades later that it becomes clear why a child did not come to birth, or survive birth, or passed as a very young child. Sometimes of course the parents may never really know on this plane.

But all parents who are paying attention will notice that their children sometimes show perceptions and abilities which seem well beyond their age capabilities .And virtually all children show signs of awareness of their chosen life task when they are very young ,before age 7.

A young man whose happiest childhood memory was colouring with crayons is now an artist. A man from an impoverished family whose happiest childhood times were spent with books becomes a teacher . A woman who wrote poems in elementary school writes for a living now.

It is of course the task of any parent to encourage their children to fulfill the destiny which their children were born to And all children show signs of what they love t in their earliest interests…a love of dancing, animals, riding a trike , running ,drawing ,looking at books , listening to stories, singing . Children within a family choose radically different roles, as Alfred Adler has indicated in this work. Even identical twins , with ostensibly identical heredity and environment , often have greatly different personalities .of course their souls are different . Our children choose us for what we can teach them about love and life task…the twin reasons for human life.

All of us are on a spiritual journey from the instant of conception until the last breath…and then, later, we start all over again.

What makes any one of us a Shaman?

An awareness that this earth plane is an illusion…As Shakespeare said, "all the world's a stage and all the men and women merely players." What is important is life task, soul mates, guides, angels, love…especially love…In fact, love is the ONLY thing that matters. It is what keeps the universe from flying apart.

Quantum physicists speak of the mysterious force which seems to connect all things, even when they are very far separated in space. All ecosystem have interconnections which we are only beginning to understand. (For most people, being in contact with unspoiled nature, where it can still be found, is a spiritual experience of All That Is.)

CHAPTER SEVENTEEN: KARMIC LAWS OF REBIRTH

China, due to a population of over one billion, has adopted a draconian one-child policy. All pregnancies must be pre-approved by local committees. Abortions are forced on women even if 8 months pregnant, if the pregnancy was not pre-approved. All city dwellers are strictly limited to one child per couple.

What counts as a child in this system? Any couple who has had a child which lives to be fifteen days old has used up its quota. They will never be allowed to have another.

Seems a little harsh for parents, doesn't it? It's harsh for babies too. Millions of girls were terminated before or after birth, because many families prefer boys. There is therefore a shortage of girls of marrying age in many regions.

As a therapist working with many couples who have lost a child at various stages, through miscarriage, termination, or death at the age of a year or two, I am often asked,

"Can this same soul come back to me?"

Well, yes and no.

The spiritual rules about soul return are just as real as the laws in China. Let's look at some examples, gleaned from hundreds of hypnotic past life regressions ,hundreds of past life channelings, and hundreds of spirit baby readings.

Rebecca had an older sister Rhonda who was stillborn. She gave birth to her own daughter (and gave her the same name) . Her mother burst into tears when she first saw the baby saying "she looks just like my Rhonda". Yes, she was the return of Rhonda.

Cornelia`s` older brother passed. When she gave birth to her own first child first she looked into his face and realised, "I know you!" Her son was the return of her brother.

A young man died in an auto accident at age 19. He had been very close to his sister . She later had three children, one of whom she named after her brother. Teresa frequently says, "He is just like Joseph!" Well actually, he IS the same spirit as Joseph.

KARMIC LAW NUMBER ONE : A deceased child, from stillbirth to young adult, can return in the NEXT generation, usually to their own sister.

My Mother in law Pauline was a delightful, very proper English lady with a penchant for matching hats and shoes…and her rocking chair. Her grandson and his wife had a shy little boy of five. Grandma often told the young couple that the little boy needed a sibling, to please make sure he wasn't lonely. They finally got pregnant just before grandma's passing.

One night I awoke from a dream of a cracked shell of an ancient queen bee, with a little young queen bee emerging from the shell. I woke my husband and said "Phyllis has passed, and she is coming back very soon." (She had in fact died during the night.)

Some months later a dying plant which I had rescued from the repo bin burst into full bloom with lovely pink flowers. "Looks like another message from Pauline, " I said. "She's going to be a girl again, and she's almost ready to return."

The baby girl Maia was extremely strong willed. Before she was a year old she insisted on choosing her own clothes, and they had to match nicely.

She was very particular about shoes, and delighted when I bought her two pairs.

When the baby was six months old and I placed her in a child's rocking chair, she looked at me intently and pushed down the arms to make it go as if to say." I remember how to do this." And very soon she became protective of her much older brother. (She also once said, "Can you help me with my buttons? Before when I was huge I could do it, but my little hands don't remember how to do it."

Her parents and remaining grandparents accept that the child is the return of her great-grandmother .

KARMIC LAW NUMBER TWO: A person who lives to be very old can return within the family several generations later.

KARMIC LAW NUMBER THREE: It is necessary for a life review to occur. However the transfer can even occur while the pregnancy is in place. A spirit baby needs to attach by age 7 weeks, but can flit in and out of the baby body, up until the instant of birth, which is the last moment to detach if it chooses to . (Although it is rare, a Spirit Baby which is attached may give up its spot to another one).

Many of my clients have had terminations for various reasons. In the case of a fetus with a severe life threatening disability which is terminated, the Spirit Baby normally says, 'It's okay mom and dad, I detached from the body and did not suffer. I am also able to come back to a healthy body when it is time."

How about miscarried babies?

The Spirit Babies routinely say, "the body was not healthy" or 'the time was not right' or "that was not the right daddy for me." They also frequently say" I never attached to the body, mommy ,and a body without a spirit baby attached by 7 weeks runs out of energy to grow."

KARMIC LAW NUMBER FOUR: When a child passes before birth the contract between parent and child has NOT been completed and the child is free to return to the same parents. In other words a child who passes before birth may return as a younger sibling.

But what about a child who passes extremely young for medical or accidental reasons. ..say, at even a few days old?

What I have been informed by the guides is that such a child may well be a spirit guide or inner child to its mother for the rest of her life...this may also occur for a terminated or miscarried child. But the contract to be a living child has been completed.

KARMIC LAW NUMBER FIVE: a child who has lived on this plane for a few days, or a couple of years, cannot return to the parents as their child. The child may become the sister's child in another generation, or a spirit guide (or inner child-source of inspiration) to a family member.

When I am working with people who are having difficulty getting pregnant, sometimes they have to "call a child in" as there is no pre-existing contract between them and a spirit baby to become parents. Where do these free-floating spirit babies come from?

Almost all Birth Contracts occur because of a previous past life connection which left unfinished business.

However, there are millions of babies who cannot return to their own soul families.

There are two reasons I know of why spirit babies may not be able to return to their own soul families.

The first is genocide. The second is killing within the family.

Members of soul families and of earthly families have a fair degree of overlap. After the Holocaust, for example, when one third of the world's Jewish people perished, the deceased souls may have had to find entirely new soul families to return to.

There were also 60,000,000 native people in the Americas prior to Columbus ; there are 800,000 now. Obviously many native souls have had to return to non–native soul families.

The aboriginal people of Australia had bounties on their heads; the elders say that the souls of those who were killed return to the families of the descendants of those who collected the bounties.

The most serious holocausts of the present time are occurring in Syria, China and India. The issue in Syria is a government killing off its own people indiscriminately. The issue in India is femicide of baby girls, as some parents do not consider a girl child to be a full member of the family; she will be married young and then belong to her husband's family, and her dowry will be expensive .In China the recently rescinded one-child policy led to millions of selective abortion of girl fetuses and female infanticide as boys were more favoured .it also led to two very large scale social problems –a huge shortage of available women fro young men to marry, ,which in any society is associated with social unrest and crime; and also a huge number of only children with two sets of grandparents who were also only children, so that there are very few young people to care for the much older ones. (A fine example of how actions and policies can have unforeseen consequences.)

A terminated child will usually forgive its parents. They can detach physically, emotionally and spiritually before the procedure.

The baby girls who were killed AFTER birth by their own parents in present-day China and India usually choose to find a whole new soul group. This is why a couple who want to call in a Spirit Baby, as they do not have a contract to have a child, have no shortage of candidates. A child may be called in by meditation. I have also assisted in calling in a spirit baby while a mother is in trance .(This does not mean the spirit baby will necessarily be a girl.)

KARMIC LAW NUMBER SIX: Usually souls incarnate within soul groups of 45-60 members, meeting the same souls over and over in different configurations. However, there are times when a soul has no family to return to, and must choose a new soul group.

KARMIC LAW NUMBER SEVEN: All souls which are not brand- new have been incarnated as different genders, races, social classes, abilities and disabilities. (Some are brand-new to human life, such as elementals.)

KARMIC LAW NUMBER EIGHT: There is a soul contract in place with many births which involves the child and at least one parent. If a person wants children they usually have a Spirit Baby in their or their partner's aura which activates this wish. People who do not want children do not have such a contract or Spirit baby. But people who DO want a baby may still have to call a Spirit Baby in.

(There are undoubtedly many reasons for the huge increase in infertility; from 6 % a generation ago to 16% now. Alongside of the obvious culprits… heavy toxic load in air, water, soil and human tissue, there is also the issue of a larger human population than at any previous time in history. Unless new souls are being created right now, presumably reincarnation has to occur much more quickly than in previous times. I do not think that my clients with fertility issues have done anything wrong; rather they are the canaries in the coal mine. Their future children usually also understand their life task very well and require parents who are already on a spiritual journey.)

CHAPTER EIGHTEEN: SOME SPIRITUAL IDEAS :PAST LIFE REGRESSION, SOUL FAMILIES, SYNCHRONICITIES, AND CHANNELING

Could you provide me with an explanation of past life regression, soul families, synchronicities and channelling? It's important or I wouldn't ask.

Certainly!

1.) **Past life regression** hypnosis is based on the understanding that souls are eternal. We are each given hundreds of lives during which we can learn from varied human experiences.

From a scientific standpoint, we know that matter and energy can neither be created or destroyed. The sum of all the matter and energy in the universe is constant, although they can change form . Although it is clear that our bodies return to dust and ashes, the life force is the most powerful component of any living being, far more than the sum of the components of minerals and water which are almost identical from species to species.

A study was done in India two decades ago about reincarnation. India was chosen because many people there are Hindu, and explicitly believe in reincarnation. They would not automatically dismiss past life memories which their children might share as being due to imagination ,as is likely to happen in other cultures .

In this study of thousands of children, many past life stories could be verified. For instance, one little girl told her parents that she had previously been a beautiful woman (she remembered her name) who liked to wear a red dress and had died in a car crash. The name of the previous home village was mentioned. It was verified as a place hundreds of miles away with which the illiterate family had no connections, and all details which the small girl gave were verified.

In another instance a child said he had lived a very long time ago in another village. He described it, with a focus on where to find the village well, which was the centre of village life. The child was taken to the village he named, and was very puzzled when the well was not where he thought it should be. But the oldest man in the village verified that his grandfather had told him there used to be a well at that spot.

Many young children in all cultures routinely speak about their past lives .However, parents in most settings dismiss this as imagination. By the age of 7-which is in the Catholic Church called the age of reason when " imagination" is no longer so strong-almost all have forgotten all they once knew when they came 'trailing clouds of glory" as William Blake expressed it .

What is the function of finding out about one's past lives? Well, there are invariably themes which the soul chooses to explore. No two souls pick exactly the same themes.

Certainly love is a central theme for virtually everyone. That is, there are many different ways of expressing love, parent – child, siblings, friends.

Of approximately equal importance is life task. Each soul brings a unique gift to the world.

One soul may incarnate over and over as some sort of artist, even when limited expression is allowed with their culture. For example, many women in cultures in which they had few creative outlets took up quilting or various forms of needlework and sewing. The Innuit, who had almost no possessions, still had beaded moccasins and made sandstone carvings and stone statues as markers.

A person whose life task was to be a storyteller might tell tales orally in one culture, be a writer in a second, and in a third might aspire to teach young adults literature at a university.

A healer might become a neurosurgeon in contemporary North America, a shaman in South America, or an herbalist in China.

Every expression of self is moderated by the gender which the soul has chosen or accepted for a lifetime, the social status of the family, and the cultural norms. Some situations are far more challenging than others, but all lives allow for opportunities to love, to learn, and to contribute to the community.

There is one belief system which states that there are 7 levels of spiritual growth, with seven steps at each level. This would imply at least 49 lives are required, but adherents of this system believe an absolute minimum of 100 lives would be necessary to learn the basics of the potential ways of being human.

In the Buddhist system a person who has actually gone through all the steps becomes a bodhisattva who does not have to reincarnate. Ironically bodhisattvas ,because of their spiritual nature, always choose to come back to help those who are still struggling .

A past life regression means just that…a person is regressed during trance first to childhood, then earlier in childhood, then to two previous lives which related to their current issues The person's own subconscious mind chooses the most relevant lives out of all the possibilities .

Almost everyone can be successfully regressed. Exceptions are extremely young children or the severely mentally challenged. But young children often spontaneously tell of past lives they remember, especially ones in which their now-parents were known to them in a different role.

The purpose of a past life regression experience is healing.

One person found that her fear of drowning was related to a previous passing as a sailor who was washed overboard during a storm. Another overcame her fear of highway driving when she re-lived a life in which she had been a stagecoach driver in England who was killed by a highwayman .

Phobias are very often rooted in past life trauma, and often start when the person reaches the same age as their previous incarnation was when the trauma occurred. So the trauma can be quickly cleared up when it is understood that it does not relate to this life. The therapist directs the person to do any forgiveness work and healing which needs to be done.

2.) Soul families

People belong to soul families of approximately 45-60 souls. That is to say, they keep reincarnating over and over and finding the same people to have relationships with. This is why love at first sight is possible, and in fact happens to most people .

But relationships are not the same from life to life. Souls fill different roles-parent-child(which is often later reversed), friend, siblings, lovers, spouses. It is all about finding different ways to love. When one feels an attraction strong enough to lead to marriage, for example, it does not mean that person was ever one's lover before...just that there was some sort of connection.

Karmic connection is caused by
-any kind of family relationship
-dying together
-any kind of love
-one causing the death of the other (this may be a partial explanation of why there are so many relationships which involve spousal abuse.)

Most people cannot differentiate at all between the types of karmic attraction which may have brought them together. So if a person loves someone who used to be their parent, it may (or may not) lead to a successful marriage.

When I was teaching kindergarten a little girl of 4 ran up to me one day and said "Mrs. Nightingale, I have something, to tell you. Before when I was big and my daddy was little, my daddy was my baby and he was in my tummy."
She just needed to be heard-she then ran off to play!

Another little girl said, "Can you help me with my buttons? Before when I was huge I used to know how to do that, but now my little fingers don't remember how." Her parents are convinced that she is the return of her own great-grandmother because they share so many personality traits.

3.) Synchronicities

Quantum physics has taught us that everything in the universe is connected, and that particles will influence each other even at astronomical distances. When things are synchronous, they occur together at the same with no causal effect being implied.

Those who believe in a beneficent universe feel that everything happens for a reason, and that we all get what we want and need if we have the right attitude.

12 years ago I decided that I had two main requirements for a home. One was a front room with a fireplace and a powder room next to that. Secondly, I wanted a huge back yard so I could be an urban farmer (bees and chickens) even though I live in a big city with (usually) very small lots.

The home I wanted appeared in the local paper the very next day. It was empty, and immediately available .

Synchronicities may sometimes be caused by an energy connection between people. Many have had the experience of thinking of a friend or relative they have not seen in years, only to have that person call them up the same day.

4.) Channeling

J. K. Rowling, author of the Harry Potter series of wildly successful children's books, was a struggling writer and single mom riding the London underground. According to her account, the entire series of 9 books was downloaded into her brain in one moment. Then she had to go home and write it all down, presumably over a period of years.

Stephen King , author or dozens of books , has stated that he writes in a trance state.

Handel's Messiah was completed in approximately 19 days of trance; Handel hardly ate or slept while he put his inspiration down on paper.

Channeling can be artistic, scientific, or spiritual. It involves tapping into the Field of All That Is.

Of course, one may spend years beforehand in preparation, but when the soul is ready to create the Theory of Relativity or the Mona Lisa or Hamlet, or to discover uranium, the person becomes a co-creator of reality, and whatever needs to come through that particular vessel, comes through.

Everyone can channel; it means creating, sometimes in a trance like state, whatever one has to give to the world .

CHAPTER NINETEEN : SPIRIT BABY SOULS AND THEMES

Most Spirit Baby souls have been around for thousands of years and have experienced both male and female bodies, many races, different social levels and cultures. Assuming that there is truth to astrological influences on a person's characteristics, a soul could certainly choose each of the zodiac signs in turn, in order to experience as many different ways of being human as possible.

I have spontaneously remembered about two dozen of my past lives –I was male in only two of them. Some of us, in other words , have a preference. Some spirit babies will wait for a female body, for example, in order to complete their life task, which might lead to a miscarriage if the parents make a body of the other gender. Others say they do not care, for this incarnation, which gender of body they have.

Certainly love is a central theme for virtually everyone. That is, there are many different ways of expressing love, parent – child, siblings, friends.

Of approximately equal importance is life task. Each soul

brings a unique gift to the world.

But what makes our souls unique? If our souls aren't male or female, and we aren't known by one identity or one face, and we can be any person, race, culture, man or woman, doesn't that make us all the same? How do we distinguish one soul from another?

Each soul explores themes. No two souls have exactly the same themes.

Themes I have explored include:

-being a healer

-being persecuted for the racial group I belonged to in several lifetimes (which I suppose I also chose as a spirit baby)

- expressing myself within the limitations of being female, which in most cultures has led to many restrictions

-finding ways to use intuitive abilities in societies which may have valued them, or may have punished them

-knowing the many different members of my soul family through many   lifetimes, in various ways

-having difficulty accepting injustice

-loving to learn in as many ways as were available

-loving animals

-being willing to die for my beliefs and convictions

-believing in creating community in any setting.

If you sat down and enumerated your main values , and
how you expressed them, even in one lifetime, you might be
able to figure out a few things about what makes you
unique... but if you had access to multiple lives(as in the
Akashic records) you might have a bigger picture of what
makes you unique. it is absolutely not based in one lifetime.
The details of gender, race, educational level, time period
 are incidental ... the themes of a given soul come up over
and over.

Christine Nightingale, B.A (Psychology, University of Toronto), Reiki Master, Hypnotist (Ontario Hypnosis Centre) Aromatherapist (Sheridan College), Spirit Baby communicator. I have helped hundreds of couples connect to their Spirit Babies ... unborn or not yet conceived children who have chosen them (which often leads to successful pregnancy.

For more info see www. nightingalehealing.com

Made in the USA
Lexington, KY
26 June 2016